What people are saying about …

UNCHAINED

"Everybody talks about freedom, but very few experience it. Still fewer have the ability to speak about it in such a refreshing, clear, and profound way. That's what Noel Heikkinen has done in the book you hold in your hands. *Unchained* is a life-changing book. You'll laugh, cry, and rejoice as you dance and sing before the throne of One who has set you free. Read this book and give it to everybody you love. They will 'rise up and call you blessed'!"

Steve Brown, seminary professor,
author, and broadcaster

"Noel writes as a pastor who is aware of the bondage men and women wrestle with. He writes out of a deep understanding of Scripture applied to real struggles in a really bound-up world. This book he has written is well worth your time."

Matt Chandler, lead pastor of
The Village Church and president of
Acts 29 Church Planting Network

"Lots of Christians talk about the incredible freedom found in the gospel, but they live their lives as if it's an idea, not a reality. In *Unchained*, Noel Heikkinen loosens the chains that keep so many who have been pardoned living like they are on probation."

Larry Osborne, pastor of North
Coast Church and author

"Recovering hypocrites of the world rejoice! Noel Jesse Heikkinen has written a beautiful primer on what may be the richest and most exciting (yet misconstrued) word in the Christian lexicon: *freedom*. Brimming with practical insight and humor, *Unchained* unpacks the infectious emancipation at the heart of the Christian faith in terms that are both enlivening and deeply reassuring. A vital contribution on a vital subject."

David Zahl, editor of *The Mockingbird Blog*
(mbird.com) and author of *A Mess of Help*

"Noel Heikkinen is one of the best new generation pastors who is effectively communicating the gospel today. Join my friend in a walk through the Scripture, his own story, and the stories of others as he helps us understand what it means to be unchained by the gospel. Read this book with a group of friends to encourage one another with his wise words."

Dave Travis, chief encouragement and
executive officer of Leadership Network

"Here is a clear, potent presentation of something I forget just about every hour of my life. The good news really is good news. But not too good to be true. Our problem is not with the message;

it's with our forgetfulness. I'm so glad for Noel, and this book. A brisk reminder of gospel liberty."

Joel Virgo, senior pastor of Church of Christ the King, Brighton, UK

"It's been said that you are only as free as those around you feel. I can't think of anyone better to write a book about our freedom in Christ than my friend Noel Heikkinen. I feel really, really free around him. As you read this book, you'll feel that freedom too. No matter where you are in your spiritual journey, I encourage you to join Noel on the path to discover the wonderful, life-changing truth contained in this simple verse: 'For freedom Christ has set us free.'"

Elliot Grudem, founder and president of Leaders Collective, pastor of Vintage Church, and author

"As a fellow 'recovering hypocrite,' I found myself feeling very hopeful as I read *Unchained*. And I was not disappointed. In his book, Noel has powerfully reminded us, in a sincere and no-nonsense way, of the freedom Jesus wants us to experience. This is a book written by a fellow traveler and not some know-it-all expert."

Chris Willard, church consultant and generosity strategist for Leadership Network and Generis

"What I like about Noel is that he's a no-nonsense, tell-it-like-it-is kind of guy. It's no surprise then that this is a no-nonsense, tell-it-like-is kind of book. Noel wants us to understand the nature of true freedom in Christ but is also clear that he wants us to actually enjoy that freedom. I gave this book to one of our members to read. She absolutely loved it. So will you!"

Steve Timmis, executive director
of Acts 29 and lead pastor of The
Crowded House, Sheffield, UK

UNCH⚒INED

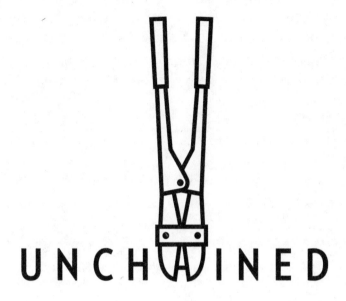

UNCHAINED

IF JESUS HAS SET US FREE,
WHY DON'T WE FEEL FREE?

NOEL JESSE HEIKKINEN

transforming lives together

UNCHAINED
Published by David C Cook
4050 Lee Vance View
Colorado Springs, CO 80918 U.S.A.

David C Cook U.K., Kingsway Communications
Eastbourne, East Sussex BN23 6NT, England

The graphic circle C logo is a registered trademark of David C Cook.

The website addresses recommended throughout this book are offered as a
resource to you. These websites are not intended in any way to be or imply an
endorsement on the part of David C Cook, nor do we vouch for their content.

Details in some stories have been changed to protect
the identities of the persons involved.

Unless otherwise noted, all Scripture quotations are taken from the ESV® Bible
(The Holy Bible, English Standard Version®), copyright © 2001 by Crossway, a
publishing ministry of Good News Publishers. Used by permission. All rights
reserved. Scripture quotations marked NIV are taken from the Holy Bible, NEW
INTERNATIONAL VERSION®, NIV®. Copyright © 1973, 2011 by Biblica, Inc.®
Used by permission. All rights reserved worldwide. NEW INTERNATIONAL
VERSION® and NIV® are registered trademarks of Biblica, Inc. Use of either
trademark for the offering of goods or services requires the prior written consent
of Biblica, Inc.; and NLT are taken from *Holy Bible*, New Living Translation,
copyright © 1996, 2007 by Tyndale House Foundation. Used by permission
of Tyndale House Publishers, Inc., Carol Stream, Illinois 60188. All rights
reserved. The author has added italics to Scripture quotations for emphasis.

LCCN 2016952724
ISBN 978-1-4347-0995-0
eISBN 978-1-4347-1001-7

Published in association with the literary agency of Mark
Sweeney & Associates, Naples, FL 34113.

The Team: Tim Peterson, Amy Konyndyk, Jack Campbell, Susan Murdock
Cover Design: Nick Lee
Cover Photos: Creative Market
Author Photo and Interior Artwork: Joshua Michels

Printed in the United States of America
First Edition 2017

1 2 3 4 5 6 7 8 9 10

111616

CONTENTS

ACKNOWLEDGMENTS

While there is customarily only one name plastered on the cover of a book, any author will tell you that writing something like this is truly a team effort. I am notoriously bad at remembering people for stuff like this, so if you were helpful to me in my writing and I forgot you, please bring me your copy of the book and I will handwrite my thanks to you on this page.

Here are the people I actually remembered to thank:

Grace (my wife)—I always say God has poured out a double portion of Grace on me, and it's true. You get the first thanks because you put up with me more than anyone. You love me well, you understand my sense of humor perfectly, and you truly know how to motivate me when I am stuck. I will always remember the day when I was feeling overwhelmed and you lovingly told me, "Suck it up and go write your book." I did. Now you have to read it. Sorry about that.

Emma, Jesse, Ethan, and Cole (my kids)—I don't know what I did to deserve you guys, but I count it as one of the great honors of my life to be your dad. Thanks for understanding why

I sat at your baseball practices and games with a manuscript in hand or stole your homework space in the office with all my stuff.

Melissa Kranzo—you are a fantastic editor and an even better friend. Thanks for jumping in at the last minute when I needed your help navigating a few sticky spots in my manuscript. You have a great talent for editing without disrupting my voice in the process. Your work on the discussion questions took this book to an entirely new level.

Fred Choi—thanks so much for the touches you added to the discussion questions in this book. I'm told it's odd to have an executive pastor who is also such a good shepherd, but I like having a bit of odd around me, so it works.

"Little" Debbie Huntley—you saw more copies of this manuscript than anyone else, as I constantly dumped stacks of pages on your desk for you to type against impossible deadlines. Nice work figuring out my handwriting—you have a rare gift.

Josh "Yoshi" Michels—thanks for your illustrative talent and creative mind. You are a consistent help for me when I get stuck, and the work that went into the illustrations in this book really helps communicate concepts that would have fallen flat if left to my words alone.

Young "Money Cash Money" Yi—thanks for all your help with research, fact checking, and the steady stream of doughnut holes, bunny ears, and Snapchats.

Mark Sweeney (my agent)—thanks for believing in this book and, more importantly, for believing in me. You gave me good shots of confidence at just the right moments for more years than I care to count.

David C Cook team—I had great fear as we dove into the editorial process on my manuscript, and I am relieved to know my trepidation was misplaced. I am very thankful for your help and guidance in putting the finishing touches on this book.

Riverview pastors—I am incredibly blessed to be surrounded by godly men like you who faithfully proclaim the liberating power of the gospel day in and day out. I love serving shoulder to shoulder with you.

And a special shout-out to Phyllis Winters, a woman from the little church I grew up in. You may not remember this, but nearly twenty years ago after hearing me preach, you shook my hand and said, "Young man, I know that I will live to see the day you write a book." It's quite possible you were the person to put this crazy idea in my head.

PART ONE

THE PROBLEM WITH CHAINS

CHAPTER 1

FREEDOM SURE DOESN'T FEEL VERY FREE

"Have you ever eaten pig brain?"

I was pretty sure something had been lost in translation. I was sitting in a restaurant in China with a new friend, and he was telling me about his favorite dish.

"Excuse me? Have I ever eaten what?"

"Pig brain," he said with precise English seasoned with a Mandarin lilt. "It's a delicacy."

When you travel internationally, you encounter moments like this when avoiding cultural offense supersedes adhering to dietary restrictions you didn't even know you had. My first thought was *There's no way I am eating that*, and up until the moment I did, a piece of my own brain held onto that conviction.

I soon learned that pig brain arrives at the table the way all other meat does in that part of the world—raw. The waiter set the plate of brain on the table, and it jiggled like undercooked tofu (which, I would learn, is also precisely how it feels on the tongue). My friend unceremoniously dumped the brain into a vat of boiling soup base simmering in the center of the table and told me to be careful not to overcook my brain.

Clearly.

A few minutes later, he plunged his chopsticks into the oily red liquid, fished out a goopy piece of brain, and tossed it into his mouth without hesitation. He then looked at me with equal parts elation and challenge in his eyes.

It was my turn.

I don't know if he believed I would do it, but I'm not one to back down from a challenge, even one as unpalatable as this. I also didn't want to be "that American" who refused to embrace new cultures. As fast as I could (so I wouldn't chicken out), I snagged a piece of brain floating in the soup, and onto my tongue it squished. The texture was, to put it politely and ironically, unnerving. It wasn't the worst thing I had ever eaten, but I probably won't go out of my way to order that particular entrée again. With great joy and a lot of laughter, we finished our meal, and somehow the chicken stomach and quail eggs we ate next seemed very tame.

Freedom tastes a lot like pig brain.

THE UNNERVING TASTE OF FREEDOM

Any self-respecting, law-abiding, faithful first-century Jew would have politely passed on my Chinese friend's meal or run for the door in disgust, but not for the same reasons I was tempted to. The Jews would have refused the dish because eating any part of a pig was a violation of the Mosaic Law (Lev. 11:7). Their revulsion would even extend to bacon. They would never touch the stuff even if it were as glorious as greasy, thick-cut, smoke-cured, pan-fried bacon.

Mmm, bacon.

Anyone who knows me well can attest to my love affair with bacon. Of course, part of me wishes I had never told my church how much I love the stuff. Don't get me wrong; I'm not ashamed of my love. It's just that nearly every gift I get from people in my church is bacon related. I am the proud owner of two bacon calendars, a "Bacon Makes Everything Better" plaque, and a stick of bacon balm—and that is just a smoky-flavored teaser of the gifts I receive on a regular basis. Here's the problem: as well intentioned as the givers are, the calendars, the plaque, and the bacon balm aren't bacon. (And don't even get me started on the travesty known as bacon chocolate.) These products certainly smell like bacon, look like bacon, and they even tell me lots of interesting facts about bacon, but they *are not bacon*!

Freedom is a lot like bacon (or pig brains if you happen to be in China). Churches like to talk about it and make calendars about it, but have they really tasted the stuff? And once they have tasted it, do they like it? Are they true to bacon, or do they flirt with bacon-themed imitations?

I have often tried to imagine the look on the apostle Peter's face the first time he tasted pork. Having grown up as Jewish as they came, he never would have touched it until he understood he was set free to do so by Jesus (Mark 7:19). Being the impetuous type, he probably ordered a BLT with the same cavalier attitude I ordered the pig brain. Did he rethink his decision when the sandwich was being made to order? Did he try to figure out how he could back out of the deal? And when it hit the table and he raised it to his lips, was it joy or terror in his eyes?

I hope there are DVRs in heaven so I can watch a replay of that first porky meal. Did he savor each foreign bite like a baby tasting ice cream for the first time? Was the stigma so grotesque to him that he reacted like a contestant on *Fear Factor* biting into a deep-fried tarantula?

For some people, truly tasting freedom for the first time can be delicious; for others, even the thought is scandalous; for still others, it can be downright scary and foreign.

That's why Kate declared, "I want to believe it, but I can't."

It wasn't the first time she had uttered those words (or similar words) in the small group that met in her living room. We had grown accustomed to Kate's internal battle, and the verse we were talking about had set her spinning again: "For freedom Christ has set us free" (Gal. 5:1). We were discussing the implications of that freedom and how God was pleased with her because of Jesus.

"God must be at least *a little bit* disappointed with me."

Disappointment is what she had come to expect. Dads can do that to a little girl, as can teachers, coaches, spouses, and schoolyard bullies. When a person is told often enough that she is worthless, it becomes hard to disagree. The older that person gets, the more this external valuation becomes internally validated. Then along comes the ultimate truth of Scripture, which says encouraging things such as, "None is righteous, no, not one … All have turned aside; together they have become worthless" (Rom. 3:10, 12).

When I first met Kate, she had synthesized this scriptural Truth (with a capital *T*) with the experiential truth (with a decidedly lowercase *t*) of her upbringing into a toxic spiritual reality. All she knew was that she was in need of saving. That's when she met Jesus. She placed her faith in Him and believed that *one day* she would be with Him forever, eternally free. Tragically, the reality of her eternal salvation didn't connect with her here and now. In this place, all she felt was His disapproving frown.

Kate believed in Jesus, and she was as devoted as they came. She met a wonderful Christian man and became an equally wonderful Christian wife and mom. But no matter how hard she tried, she couldn't shake this nagging feeling that God was tallying up her missteps, tsk-tsking every time she slipped up. *Eternal* forgiveness didn't mean she was let off the hook *today*. Every day Kate walked around with heavy chains around her soul, and she's not the only one.

Robert can't kick his porn habit and feels as though he wears a scarlet letter ever since it ruined his marriage.

Emily wonders if the history of past relationships dutifully recorded in her journal, memory, and bed have made her "spoiled goods" to any guy she meets in church.

Phil is haunted by his alcoholism even though he is seventeen years sober.

Jennifer laments her atrocious prayer life that consists of no more than ninety seconds on a good day before her mind is overcome by her monstrous to-do list and screaming toddler.

Chains have become so much a part of our daily existence that we don't even know that we are weighed down.

I certainly didn't.

NOEL, THE RECOVERING HYPOCRITE

I grew up in a fantastic Christian home in which my parents took me to a faithful, Bible-believing church. We went to Sunday school and VBS regularly, and I had the perfect-attendance stickers to prove it. I preached my first sermon as a middle schooler (my mom wrote it for me) and became president of the youth group when I was in high school (I still don't know why we needed officers). All of this was just enough to satisfy any doubts anyone may have had that I was saved. But there was just this one little problem: I was a hypocrite. I went to school one town over from where I lived and went to church. In this town, I could do what I wanted with whomever I wanted whenever I wanted … and I did. I wasn't a super-rebellious kid, but anyone who really knew me would have seen the disconnect between what I said I believed and how I lived my life.

If that wasn't enough, there was an even bigger problem: I didn't know there was anything wrong with living two lives, at least not consciously. I had somehow caught the notion that a Christian's spiritual life was something he did at church or when he was around his mom and dad. When around his friends, he could drop the act. However, in my case, I had friends who went to the same church I did, so I had to subconsciously and delicately keep my worlds apart. I couldn't very well have my girlfriend show up at church; that would have quite literally spoiled all the fun. Let's just say I recognize the look in couples' eyes when they come to church together after a night ... together.

Looking back, I am not sure how my conscience didn't connect the dots, but this life I was living was, for all intents and purposes, perfect. So perfect. Sin was fun, and I was (and am) a great sinner. Armed with years of hypocritical experience, off I went to college. As a seventeen-year-old freshman at Michigan State University, I settled into the same duplicitous pattern I was so well versed in, but this time, it backfired—big time. Apparently, you can't have Bible studies on the same dorm floor where the girl you are trying to score with lives. My freshman year was a complete and utter waste. I crashed and burned academically, financially, relationally, and spiritually. I was one of the youngest people to become a leader in the campus ministry I was part of and, just as notably, one of the fastest booted off the team for living an immoral lifestyle.

The summer between my first and second freshman years, I went to Africa on a mission trip that also served as a convenient way to escape the wrath of my dad when my grade reports, parking tickets, and credit-card statements arrived. That summer, I determined to crack open the Bible to read the thing for myself. This time, I wasn't just going to read a verse here and a verse there. I wanted to know what it really meant to be a Christian and what the church was supposed to look like. I decided that I would read every word of the New Testament and log what I found. What I discovered on those pages was Jesus, and He blew my mind. He was radical and demanded everything of His followers. He didn't just die on the cross, but He asked His followers to pick up their own crosses and follow Him (Matt. 16:24). He talked a little bit about heaven (Matt. 6:19–21; John 14:2) and a lot about hell (Matt. 13:41–42, 49–50; Mark 9:43). I'm not sure if this is when I truly placed my faith in Jesus or if it was one of the dozen times before, but this time it stuck. I knew it stuck because from that point forward, I felt guilty about *everything*.

I pretty quickly went back to my vice and continued to date around until a non-Christian girl I was treating way too casually called me out on my hypocrisy. Yes, you read that right; my non-Christian fling told me I wasn't living as a Christian should. And I knew it too! Every time we went out, my conscience would flare up and I would fight to keep the Holy Spirit in check.

I was free, but I sure didn't feel free. Now that I was back to my so-called perfect double life, I found that I felt really bad about it. Somehow freedom didn't taste as good as I thought it would. The problem was that I was living a counterfeit freedom, like bacon-flavored toothpaste.

There was no joy in my sin, and I felt trapped.

That's when I stumbled onto the same verse that tripped up Kate in our small group: "For freedom Christ has set us free" (Gal. 5:1). As respectfully as I can say it, this initially sounded like a bunch of bull. Freedom? I felt freer before I started taking my faith seriously! Was I missing something? And it wasn't as though I could ask anyone about it, because it seemed like everyone I knew had it together.

Little did I know, they were thinking the same thing about me. That's why I often refer to myself as a "recovering hypocrite." Perhaps others will be able to look at my life and realize they don't need to fake it anymore either. We are in this together, desperately trying to figure what freedom in Christ really means.

THE BIG QUESTION

Full disclosure time.

The reason I am writing this book is because I have heard variations of the same question time and time again, from the church lobby to the hotel bar: "If Jesus has set us free, why aren't we?"

At the risk of sounding condescending, have you read the verse I keep quoting? Really read it? Slowly? Every single word?

> For freedom Christ has set us free. (Gal. 5:1)

In this short verse, the apostle Paul is arguing that Jesus Christ has set us free and the whole point of our freedom is … wait for it … freedom! If this is true (and it is), freedom ought to be one of the defining marks of a follower of Jesus. Just like my wedding ring tells the world I am married, freedom should tell the world I am Christian.

When Paul wrote these words, he was writing to Christians who were facing a specific false teaching. They were being told that the way you could identify a true Christian was the same way you could identify a Jew: they were circumcised. The false teachers' argument was simple: "No circumcision? No Jesus." Paul took these guys to task (too late for some of his readers who had rushed out to get a quick snip) and taught emphatically that a Christian's marking was not a physical one but a spiritual one. The way you could identify a Christian was that he was free!

Freedom was the reason Jesus came to earth (Matt. 1:23–25), lived a sinless life (1 Pet. 2:22), died on the cross (Luke 23:46), was buried (vv. 52–53), rose again (24:6), and ascended into heaven (v. 51). He did it all to set the captives free (4:18). Even more astonishing was that the reason Jesus set us free was so we would actually be free!

No freedom? No Jesus!

Paul's entire argument in Galatians is that freedom is both the means and the end of the Christian life. It's what we get and what we become. It's who we are because of Jesus. We are free!

DON'T LET ANYONE STEAL YOUR FREEDOM

Because both the means and the end of the Christian life is freedom, because freedom is the reason Jesus came, Paul uses incredibly strong language to talk about a proper response to those who try to steal Christians' freedom from them: "For freedom Christ has set us free; stand firm therefore, and do not submit again to a yoke of slavery" (Gal. 5:1).

"Stand firm" is a military term that is brilliantly illustrated in the movie *300*. In one iconic scene, the Spartans line up shield to shield in a small crevice while an opposing army that vastly outnumbers them thunders toward their position. Knowing a mass of humanity is about to crash into them, they stand firm. Leonidas, the king of Sparta, yells, "Hold!" When their front line is hit, it is hit hard, but the soldiers stand firm.

That's precisely what Paul is commanding those who have been set free by Jesus. Our freedom is at stake, and there is a great opposing force that is hell bent on putting us back in chains. They will stop at nothing to make sure our faith feels like slavery. Paul, like a Spartan commander, declares, "Hold!"

But what is this overwhelming enemy in Paul's imagery?

Is it the entirety of the Roman Empire? No. It's a much stronger force.

Is it sin? Nope.

Is it Satan or his demons? Surprisingly, no.

Death? No. Death is no match for our freedom, for then we will be truly free forever.

What could it be?

The force that brutally opposes those who have been set free by Jesus is other so-called Christians, specifically those who claim to follow Jesus but try to enslave the very people Jesus has set free.

When faced with this foe, Paul commands, "Stand firm and do not submit to a yoke of slavery." What is a yoke of slavery? Paul's early readers would have been familiar with two definitions of *yoke*.

The first was a set of rules established by a rabbi. The idea was simple. Sin is bad, and people should stay as far away from it as possible. Therefore, to keep people from sin, they should stay away from anything that might tempt them to sin. But some teachers didn't stop there. They wanted to make sure people stayed away from anything that might tempt them to be tempted to sin. And on and on the rule creation would go. Jewish teachers would become known for these symbolic fences they built around the Law, and their new sets of rules would be known as their "yoke."

The second type of yoke was a device a farmer would place between a weak animal and a strong one to keep the weaker in line. When you combine the two definitions, the message of these false teachers is clear: "You are a weak animal. You know what you should do and you don't do it. You know, as a follower of Jesus, your standard is His life and teaching. You know you cannot plow in a straight line no matter how hard you try." The solution they had to this problem was a yoke, complete with rules and regulations that went above and beyond Scripture, that they would place around people's necks to keep them in line.

WHAT'S THE PROBLEM WITH YOKES ANYWAY?

I am a die-hard Apple user, and I wrote the first draft of this manuscript on my trusty MacBook using Apple Pages. Unfortunately, my publisher uses Microsoft Word. Therefore, in violation of my conscience, I had to convert everything over. While I was begrudgingly installing the Microsoft Office Suite and figuring out how to use it, this message popped up in the tutorial: "Freedom can be scary without structure."

Microsoft just perfectly described why Christians struggle with their freedom. We are afraid. We don't have control. We structure our spiritual lives in such a way that we can monitor and measure how we are doing and, presumably, how God feels about us at any given moment.

Take our prayer lives, for example. We all know that prayer is important and that we should pray. We've heard the sermons and the stories of "prayer warriors" like my own mom, who dedicates days to prayer and once went from full-time to part-time work so she could pray more. Yet most Christians I have met would tell you their prayer lives are atrocious. It's not that we don't want to pray. We really do.

So what do we do? We create a structured prayer life.

We download an app that tracks prayer requests, and we commit to praying every day. Usually, we do great for several days, but then we miss one. And what is our reaction to our forgetfulness? We beat ourselves up—not because we didn't pray, but because we didn't follow our man-made prayer structure. Our attempt to pray ends up making us feel worse about our prayer lives.

What about reading the Bible? As Christians, we know the Bible is how God communicates with us, and most of us have, at one time or another, made a commitment to read it every day. But then we miss a day and we feel God is disappointed with us and will not help us with anything that day. We are on our own for the next twenty-four hours because of our massive failure of not reading a few verses before breakfast.

Now, is a prayer app a bad thing? No! I have one and use it (sort of). Is a Bible-reading plan a bad thing? I hope not—our church has one, and we encourage people to use it. The problem occurs when our man-made rules become more important than Jesus—when praying or reading the Bible every day becomes more important than following Jesus. But wait, aren't they the same thing? No!

The Word of God is essential, but until the printing press was invented in 1440, most people didn't have their own copy. They couldn't read it every day even if they wanted to. Does that mean the Christians who lived before 1440 were lesser Christians than we are?

What about prayer? We should certainly pray—we are even told to "pray continually" (1 Thess. 5:17 NIV)—but there are no commands in Scripture about precisely how that is to play out in our lives. And if you are tempted to just repeat the Lord's Prayer over and over, remember that Jesus Himself slammed rote, robotic prayers in Matthew 6.

The problem with yokes is that they go beyond the point of where Scripture goes and demand more than Scripture demands. They place chains on our souls, and then, in a deadly twist, the rules we come up with become the measuring stick of our faith and how we think God feels about us. When we fail at our rules, we don't feel free.

That doesn't mean we aren't free. *It just means that even though you cannot lose your freedom, you can lose feeling free.*

OUR MISERABLE FAITH

Have you ever noticed that so many Christians seem miserable? I'm not talking about the fake smiles they plaster on their faces when they pull into the church parking lot. I mean the real them they put on when they drive away. It's not just the churchgoers who don't feel free either. I know solid Christians who are miserable. They think of all that Jesus did for them; they imagine the torture He endured, the crown of thorns jammed onto His head, and the spear thrust into His side. The brutality and humiliation of the cross makes them think, *The least I can do to pay Jesus back is ...* And that's where things go sideways. We think we have to pay at least a little of the price for our salvation or at least have something in our lives to show for it.

We want something to tell the world "I am a Christian," and we think we have to manufacture it somehow. We want a marking.

Paul says we already have one. "For freedom Christ has set us free."

So why don't we feel free?

Maybe the first problem is we don't even know what freedom is from a biblical perspective. As Americans, we think we have a corner on freedom, living in the land of the free and all. But because we look at freedom from the narrow perspective of our political landscape, we think of it as one of our "rights."

Recently, both guns and gay marriage have been in the news. Gun owners demand the right to keep and carry firearms, and gay couples demand the right to marry whomever they wish, and these two issues give a glimpse into our definition of freedom. For us, *free is all about me*. Let me say it a different way: we think being free means being left alone to do whatever we want. Bruce Ware, in his book *Father, Son, and Holy Spirit*, reminds us:

> Freedom is not what our culture tells us it is. Freedom is *not* my deciding, from the urges and longings of my sinful nature, to do *what* I want to do, *when* I want to do it, *how* I want to do it, *with whom* I want to do it. According to the Bible, that is bondage, not freedom.[1]

It's like all of those disgusting bacon-related, non-bacon imitations. They have a baconesque flavor, but they aren't bacon!

The problem is that we carry this faulty definition of freedom into the Bible, and things get sticky because that's not what Paul is talking about when he says, "For freedom Christ has set us free." It's so much bigger and better.

DISCUSSION QUESTIONS

Describe when you first experienced freedom. What was your first taste like? Was it delicious, scandalous, or scary? Or have you never experienced it at all?

Do you relate to Kate in her doubt of God's approval? Or to the author's description of himself as a "recovering hypocrite"?

When you think of the Christians you know, is freedom one of their defining characteristics? Is it for you?

Would you say your spiritual walk feels more like freedom or slavery?

What are some of the "yokes" or structures that you've created in your life or that you've felt are necessary to adhere to? How has applying these to your life worked out?

Discuss our culture's definition of freedom and how that compares to the biblical definition. How are they the same? How are they different?

CHAPTER 2

REALLY FREE BUT NOT REALLY FREE

Anyone who travels frequently is probably familiar with an interesting phenomenon. As you prepare for a trip, you form a picture in your mind of what the place you are traveling to is going to be like. Pictures you have seen, stories you have heard, and your imagination itself all add to the narrative. But without fail, when you arrive at your destination, it is never what you expected it to be. Sometimes it's worse, sometimes it's better, but it is always *different*. Later, when you think about your trip, the memories of these places are richer and more complete than the imagined ones could ever be.

When I recall stepping off the plane in Kenya, I immediately feel the humidity and laugh at the chickens I saw on the runway (no kidding).

When I think of riding in a taxicab through a massive city in China, I remember vividly the smog being so thick I couldn't see the tops of the skyscrapers or take a breath without wondering about the damage I was inflicting on my lungs just by being there.

When I see images of the Eiffel Tower, I smile as I remember that every hour after dark it lights up and sparkles for a few minutes—as did my daughter's face every time she saw it.

Now, if you have been to any of these places yourself, you immediately know what I am talking about. You and I have been there in person—we've experienced it. If you haven't, no matter how much you conjure up your best mental picture, you're missing some crucial piece.

This is one of the core issues when it comes to living in our freedom fully: we don't know what we don't know. We may have heard a description of the freedom we have in Christ, we've read about it in the Bible, we've heard sermons about it, or we've read a fantastic book about it (ahem). But we are limited in our ability to really, truly grasp it because our freedom exists in a place we have never been.

This is most clearly betrayed in our overly simplistic belief that freedom means *being able to do whatever we want*. Thinking that makes sense because our minds cannot fully comprehend anything else; our experience limits what we can imagine.

Let me say it a different way: *what we want is the problem because we don't know how to want something else.*

Perhaps a picture will help.

See the little guy in the bottom-left-hand corner? That's you! The entire world you can comprehend fits neatly in the box. It's filled with memories, experiences, people, biases, successes, failures, the taste of red licorice, the roar of a monster-truck rally, everything!

See where God is? Yeah … He's outside the box, sitting on His throne. He's actually *way outside the box*, but I didn't have a big enough piece of paper to sketch that out for you. Now (you're going to have to use your imagination here) the walls of this box are made of one-way mirrors. God can see in, but we can't see out. All we see when we try to look out of the box is ourselves and the other stuff that is in the box with us. That means our world, inside the box, is by its very nature self-centered. We can't help it. We're stuck in here, chained to the bottom of the box.

That's not even the big problem. It gets worse because we aren't in this box alone. The air we breathe in this box is infected with a virus the Bible calls "sin." We're going to get into sin a lot more in the next chapter, but for now, let's introduce a simple definition.[1]

Sin is any failure to reflect the image of God in nature, attitude, or action.

In less theological terms, you could say sin is any time we are unlike God in any way. Tragically, since God is outside the box and we are trapped inside, breathing in sin, everything we can conceive of is tainted and is at its core *ungodlike*.

We can see how different we are from God based on a few descriptions of Him in the Bible.

> God is love. (1 John 4:8)

Notice this doesn't say God is lov*ing* or lov*able*. It says He *is* love. Love is the very essence of God. Now, I have been known to have my lovable moments, and I can be loving on occasion, but you'd have to be seriously deluded to say I *am* love. I haven't met anyone who fits that bill. So because God *is love*, any time we do something unloving, think something unloving, or channel our inner jerk, we sin.

> Jesus Christ is the same yesterday and today and forever. (Heb. 13:8)

Does this mean Jesus is as boring as a person who eats a bowl of oatmeal and a banana for breakfast every day? No, it means Jesus is perfectly internally and externally consistent, free from mixed motives. Can that be said of you? Not of me! Yep, you guessed it; that means we are sinful in our crazy inconsistency.

> For [God's] anger is but for a moment, and his
> favor is for a lifetime (Ps. 30:5)

I don't know about you, but my anger usually lasts a wee bit longer than a moment. When someone does me wrong, my default mode is to hang on to that little nugget of emotion so I can unleash it back at the person who hurt me when he or she least expects it. If anything is "but a moment," it's my favor.

Now we could look at verses like this for the rest of the book, but it is pretty apparent: we are fundamentally unlike God. That means that even our greatest moments of godlikeness are an instantaneous flash, and when we become aware of them, they are gone in an avalanche of pride. And this isn't something we can get ourselves out of either. Remember our definition of sin? It's not just our attitudes and actions that trap us in the box; it's our very nature! We are, at the core of our being, unlike God. That means we are most comfortable in the box. We sit in here, heavy chains wrapped around our souls, and because this is all we have ever known, we settle in for the long haul.

What does this have to do with freedom? Everything! If we are most comfortable in the box, our hopes, dreams, aspirations, and *all the things we want to be free to do* are also in here with us.

Therein lies the problem.

When the Bible tells us, "For freedom Christ has set us free," our only conceivable version of that freedom is logically whatever we can conceive of. That means our sin doesn't just keep us from God—it keeps us from grasping a vision for what it means to be free.

In 1 Corinthians 13, Paul grappled with this reality when he wrote, "For now we see in a mirror dimly, but then face to face. Now I know in part; then I shall know fully, even as I have been fully known" (v. 12). He was saying our ability to grasp and know God, and therefore all that He has offered us, is stymied by the box.

Earlier in 1 Corinthians, Paul quoted the prophet Isaiah, who wrote:

> What no eye has seen, nor ear heard,
>   nor the heart of man imagined,
> what God has prepared for those who love
>   him. (2:9)

Paul was reminding the Corinthians that no one saw Jesus coming. No one could wrap their heads around God becoming man, the virgin birth, His miracles, or anything related to what Jesus was, said, or did. His own disciples seemed to wrestle with this for three years—and they had direct access to Him all day every day! Even with the myriad of prophecies in the Old Testament, even with Jesus plainly declaring His death and resurrection, they could not fathom what Jesus was going to do. They certainly didn't see Him taking a detour to the cross for the sins of the world instead of heading straight to His earthly throne in Jerusalem.

Why not?

Because they were in the box!

No one's eyes had ever seen someone do what Jesus was going to do. Their ears hadn't heard anything like it either. Even their imaginations were stuck inside the box. Imagine how difficult it would be to tell sinful human beings that God Himself would put humanity onto His deity without losing it in the process, would resist all temptation without tapping into His divine nature, would willingly die a brutal death, and would be able to raise Himself from the dead! It would be like trying to explain GPS to Lewis and Clark. Or describing cruise control to Alexander the Great. Or explaining Snapchat to your uncle Al, who can't even get the hang of operating his toaster oven.

It's impossible!

If no one could conceive of what Jesus was going to accomplish when He came to earth the first time, it continues to be true for what He is doing now and what He will do when He comes to earth the second time. Just try to read the book of Revelation!

Our brains are stymied trying to grapple with Jesus, which means we are equally stymied trying to comprehend the true freedom He offers.

We've never seen anything like it!

So what do we do? Is all hope of freedom lost? No!

"For freedom Christ has set us free" is not a lie. We are free, and we can experience it.

GRAPPLING WITH THE BOX

The best way to begin wrestling with our chained state is to remember: even though we are in the box, we are no longer in the box. No, that's not a typo. If you have been saved by grace through faith in Jesus, you are both in the box and not in the box.

Christians have an enormous number of new realities they are faced with. Here are a few:

> [God the Father] *has delivered us* from the domain
> of darkness and *transferred us* to the kingdom of
> his beloved Son, in whom we have redemption,
> the forgiveness of sins. (Col. 1:13–14)

Did you see it?

You have *already* been delivered from the domain of darkness. You have *already* been transferred into Jesus's kingdom. You *already* have a new citizenship, you *already* have a new king, you are *already* playing for a new team. You have been plucked out of one kingdom (box) and placed into another (outside the box). It's a done deal.

> *And you were dead in the trespasses and sins in*
> *which you once walked*, following the course of
> this world, following the prince of the power
> of the air, the spirit that is now at work in the
> sons of disobedience—among whom we all once

lived in the passions of our flesh, carrying out the
desires of the body and the mind, and *were by
nature children of wrath, like the rest of mankind.
But God, being rich in mercy, because of the great
love with which he loved us, even when we were
dead in our trespasses, made us alive together with
Christ—by grace you have been saved—and raised
us up with him and seated us with him in the heavenly places in Christ Jesus, so that in the coming ages
he might show the immeasurable riches of his grace
in kindness toward us in Christ Jesus.* (Eph. 2:1–7)

There it is again! You *were* dead; you *were* by very nature
children of wrath. But something happened. God *made* you alive,
God *saved* you, God *raised you up*, and my personal favorite: God
seated you with Him in the heavenly places. You were chained in the
box, but now you are set free, sitting outside of the box with God.
That's where you are right now!

Okay. Stop and put the book down for a second and look
around. I'll wait.

Does it look like you are sitting in the heavenly places?

Unless you are reading this in Wrigley Field where the Chicago
Cubs are winning the seventh game of the World Series, your
answer is probably no.[2] We get glimpses of heaven here on earth,
but most of the time, sin's weight is still very real. What gives? The
reality is that you are not only outside of the box, but you are also
still very much inside the box.

It's a paradox.

Theologians call these two states we exist in simultaneously our "position" and our "condition."

Our position is we are seated with Jesus in the heavenly places, perfect and righteous in God's sight.

Our condition is we are still here on earth, struggling with the very sin we have already been set free from.

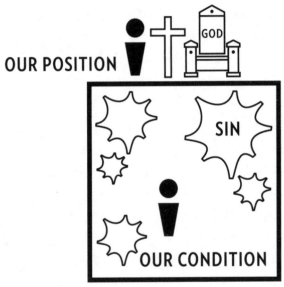

There aren't two of you (even though the diagram shows two of you). Rather, you are in both places at the same time.

Tragically, most people spend all of their time (or most of it) focused on their condition rather than their position. They futilely try to look outside of the box from the inside, which invariably leads to them spending too much time looking at themselves and their sin. They end up feeling trapped inside the box. And then someone tells them, "For freedom Christ has set us free," and they don't get it. This life doesn't feel very free.

THE BOX HAS A CLAW

I was taking a tour of a building our church was purchasing when I came across something unexpected: a claw machine. As I tried to figure out what it was doing in a church, I realized that right there in front of me, in all of its carnival glory, was a beautiful picture of the gospel.

Imagine for a moment that the box we have been talking about is actually a claw machine. Every one of us is piled up in the bottom, an assortment of odd prizes, each with value only in the eye of the machine operator who is (obviously) outside of the claw machine. Our path out of the machine is a chute that we are utterly incapable of reaching on our own. But there, hanging above our heads, is our savior: the claw. Every so often, the claw goes on the prowl, controlled by a seemingly invisible force. It slides this way and that way and then settles in over our heads. Suddenly, it descends and the shiny chrome-plated claw grabs onto us … sorta. We feel like we are going to slip out of its clutches, but up we go to the top of the machine, where, for a fraction of a second, we stop and begin to swing violently. A second later, we begin the herky-jerky journey to the chute, swinging, swinging, sliding, sliding. At just the right time, we are dropped into the chute and slide out of the machine forever.

This is what it feels like to be a follower of Jesus. In a sense, we are still inside the box, but our new reality is that we have been securely snatched from it and are on our way out. On the journey, which feels like a lifetime … because it is, God asks us to trust that we are secure in the claw.

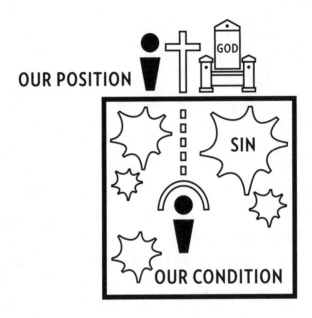

But hanging there doesn't feel very secure, does it? So we do what comes naturally: we panic.

We don't trust the claw, and we try to take matters into our own hands. In the precious seconds between being snatched from this evil age and dropped into the eternal age, we try to make ourselves more secure.

STRAPPING OURSELVES TO THE CLAW

You see, as sinners, we come to Jesus all messed up and we place our faith in Him to save us because we know we can't do it on our own. The problem arises when we shift into human-effort mode. Why do we do it? Because we want to be "good Christians." We want to "mature." We want to "grow." These are all good things, but we have to consider what motivates us to do them.

If we were honest, for many of us, it's really about other people. We want to *look like* good Christians. We are insecure about where we are in our spiritual journey, and we want to look good. We make goals and resolutions and plans centered on what other people will see in us.

Others of us are just trying to make God happy. We want Him to say "I am pleased" when He looks at our lives. Every day we feel the tension between what God desires from His people and how we know we are living, and we can't imagine He likes what He sees. But don't forget this beautiful truth: because of Jesus, because of His death, burial, and resurrection, *God is already pleased with those He has rescued from the box.*

I am a big fan of Christmas, with all the decorations and trappings, and I love the tradition of going out to a tree farm with my family, cutting down some nature, and bringing it into my house. For the first decade or so of my marriage, I was always afraid the tree was going to fly off my van during the ride home, so I would really tie it down. I brought my own bungee cords, and I would tie some twine to the tree branches. I was the same way with rooftop luggage racks. I was always afraid our luggage would end up on the highway somewhere, so I would add lots of extra straps across the top. It was annoying, the way the straps would slap the roof in the wind, but at least I knew something was still up there.

That's what we do with Jesus … or rather, the claw. To feel secure in the claw, we strap ourselves in. We do stuff that we are sure will help us make it to the chute. And here's the biggest problem: just like my Christmas trees and luggage racks, sometimes it appears to work! When we succeed in our goals, resolutions, and plans, we begin to see them as the cause (instead of Jesus), and then we try to put those straps on other people. If it worked for us, it'll work for them, right?

Wrong.

The straps aren't doing anything except making us feel better; all we've done is replace our chains with straps.

After a decade or so, I realized that the makers of luggage racks were confident in their built-in roof-attaching mechanisms. Why wasn't I? I began watching other dads tie just a couple of ropes to their trees and not have any problems. Huh. It turned out I was adding some really unnecessary stuff to my life.

Not a century goes by in church history without some group trying to add something to the faith and declaring they have found the answer to "true Christianity," or at least a more faithful Christianity.

I went through an "I should pray for an hour a day" (see Matt. 26:40) phase and an "I should listen to only Christian music" phase (see Eph. 5:19) in my Christian walk. I know people who swear by a daily quiet time in the morning (Ps. 5:3) and others who like to spend time praying at night (Ps. 119:62). All of these are great things, but they do not attach you any more firmly to the claw.

The truth is that I have never met anyone who added any of these little rules to their lives because they were trying to negate the grace of God. On the contrary, they usually develop these practices in order to be more faithful followers of Jesus. They usually have a verse to back up their newfound conviction too (that's why I listed a few in the last paragraph).

But there is a moment when these great things lose their greatness, and that is when you (almost inevitably) look at another Christian and say, "Your Christian walk would be better *if you did what I do*."

But really, what harm is there in adding a few little rules? Isn't that okay or at least a little helpful? Not according to Paul!

> I am astonished that you are so quickly deserting him who called you in the grace of Christ and are turning to a different gospel—not that there is another one, but there are some who trouble you and want to distort the gospel of Christ. (Gal. 1:6–7)

Here is Paul's concern. When you add little rules to your faith (even good ones) and begin to call them essential to a mature Christian walk, you are unwittingly deserting Jesus! In military terms, you are going AWOL. When *how* you follow Jesus becomes more important than actually following Him, it's as though you are deserting your commanding officer and signing up to fight for another army.

I once heard someone answer a common question—"How does God feel toward me when I sin?"—with the answer, "Exactly how He felt toward Jesus when He did not sin." Does that bother you? That's because you are more comfortable with chains (just like our friend Kate back in chapter 1). Does this mean we have a license to sin? We can do whatever we want? No. We'll get there later in this book. For now, suffice it to say that the Bible is clear on what God expects of His followers. We don't have a license to lie, to cheat, to steal, to mistreat the poor, to be greedy, or to have sex with someone we aren't married to.

But the reality when we sin (which we will, repeatedly) is that it's already been dealt with. Jesus already took those sins to the cross. And if we truly believe in Him, our chains are broken and we are set free.

Truly free.

For freedom Christ has set us free. (Gal. 5:1)

If you decide to finish reading this book, you are going to get seriously tired of this verse. Either that or you are going to love it and want to get it tattooed somewhere obvious. It could really go either way.

Maybe this is why the apostle Paul starts all of his letters with the gospel and then, once he has reminded us of all we have in Jesus, *only then* does he move to how the gospel weaves its way into the rest of our lives. We are secure in the claw first, and that is the most important thing. So let's work through this the same way Paul does by starting with the gospel.

> Grace to you and peace from God our Father and the Lord Jesus Christ, who gave himself for our sins to deliver us from the present evil age, according to the will of our God and Father, to whom be the glory forever and ever. Amen. (Gal. 1:3–5)

This is the message of the gospel, or dare I say, the "gospel claw." Paul's statement is meant to give his readers a sense of security. This is where that security comes from: *after living a sinless life, Jesus Christ died (gave Himself for our sins) and was raised from the dead.* Without His death and His resurrection, we do not have Christianity. These are not negotiable doctrines. The fact that He did this for our sins is not a negotiable doctrine. Jesus wasn't just a good moral teacher, and He wasn't just a great example: He was our scapegoat. Our sins were piled on Him. He died so we might live. That is the gospel, and it is *literally* all we need to be secure.

Read this list of verses and think about who is actually at work:

> But you are a chosen race, a royal priesthood, a holy nation, a people for his own possession, that you may proclaim the excellencies of him who

called you out of darkness into his marvelous light. Once you were not a people, but now you are God's people; once you had not received mercy, but now you have received mercy. (1 Pet. 2:9–10)

God is faithful, by whom you were called into the fellowship of his Son, Jesus Christ our Lord. (1 Cor. 1:9)

Therefore do not be ashamed of the testimony about our Lord, nor of me his prisoner, but share in suffering for the gospel by the power of God, who saved us and called us to a holy calling, not because of our works but because of his own purpose and grace, which he gave us in Christ Jesus before the ages began. (2 Tim. 1:8–9)

Blessed be the God and Father of our Lord Jesus Christ, who has blessed us in Christ with every spiritual blessing in the heavenly places, even as he chose us in him before the foundation of the world, that we should be holy and blameless before him. In love he predestined us for adoption to himself as sons through Jesus Christ, according to the purpose of his will, to the praise of his glorious grace, with which he has blessed us in the Beloved. (Eph. 1:3–6)

Look at all these active verbs: He *called* us, He *saved* us, He *chose* us, He *predestined* us. God is actively involved in every aspect of our salvation. It's really crazy to think about, but before He spun the world into existence, God had us in mind and He had already made up His mind to save us. It wasn't as if He had to scramble to think of something to do to fix all that we had messed up.

The gospel isn't "plan B." Grabbing you with the claw and dropping you into the chute of eternal life has always been "plan A." Before you even dreamed up that terrible sin you think God can't forgive, your salvation was a done deal. And because salvation is all about God, He gets all the glory. As Paul put it, salvation "is not your own doing; it is the gift of God, not a result of works, so that no one may boast" (Eph. 2:8–9).

In his fantastic book *Gospel*, J. D. Greear wrote these words: "Christ's obedience is so spectacular there is nothing we could do to add to it; His death so final that nothing could take away from it."[3] Through Jesus's spectacular obedience and final death, we are set free.

Completely free.

This is how secure you are in your freedom:

> For I am sure that neither death nor life, nor angels nor rulers, nor things present nor things to come, nor powers, nor height nor depth, nor anything else in all creation, will be able to separate us from the love of God in Christ Jesus our Lord. (Rom. 8:38–39)

That's a pretty remarkable list, and it includes everything that has ever been created (yourself included). And everything on that list is powerless to separate you from the claw. This sucker isn't rigged. If Jesus has saved you, you are safe and secure. Even though you are dangling inside the evil world of the claw machine, there is no way you will ever be dropped. In fact, at the risk of completely destroying our metaphor, let's reimagine the claw as a titanium-reinforced, hermetically sealed, nuclear-weapon-proof elevator with doors that will not open until we have cleared this world and made it to the next.

That's the gospel, and it's why Paul is concerned that we "are turning to a different gospel—not that there is another one." There is only one gospel! Everything else is a false gospel. Now don't forget what *gospel* means. It means "good news." There is only one set of good news!

Earlier I mentioned that a robust understanding of the gospel is essential to us feeling free, and here it is: Jesus Christ's sinless life, death, burial, and resurrection have set us free. Everything else is bad news. "Humanism" is bad news because it says it is all about us instead of Jesus. "Try Harder Religion" is bad news because it says Jesus's sacrifice wasn't enough. Any so-called gospel that takes work out of Jesus's hands and gives it to anyone else is a distortion of the gospel of Christ.

Paul even laid out a hypothetical situation.

> But even if we or an angel from heaven should preach to you a gospel contrary to the one we preached to you, let him be accursed. As we have

said before, so now I say again: If anyone is preaching to you a gospel contrary to the one you received, let him be accursed. (Gal. 1:8–9)

He was like, "If I came in and said, 'I was wrong; you should follow this new gospel now,' I should be cursed." In Romans 9, Paul used the same word to describe someone who wasn't even a Christian! He then said the same thing about angels. If an angel from heaven appeared on the scene, shining brightly, and he declared a new gospel, he was to be accursed. And then Paul was like, "In case you missed it, let me say it again: 'As we have said before, so now I say again: If anyone is preaching to you a gospel contrary to the one you received, let him be accursed.'"

Freedom is *that* big of a deal.

DISCUSSION QUESTIONS

Freedom does *not* mean being able to do whatever we want and "what we want is the problem because we don't know how to want something else." Talk about what this means.

Living in the box, not only apart from God but also infected with sin, might seem discouraging to consider. What is your first reaction to this idea? Is it a new concept to you or something you've thought about before?

Discuss your *position* (with God, perfect and righteous in His eyes) versus your *condition* (on earth struggling with the sin you have been set free from). Which one would you say you spend most of your time focused on?

What motivates you to want to grow and mature in Christ? Is it ever to appear a certain way to others or to try to gain God's approval?

Do you believe that God is already entirely pleased with you, *no matter what you do*?

What are some of the straps you've put on yourself in an attempt to secure or preserve your salvation? What goals, resolutions, or plans seem to work for you? Are these necessary? Helpful? Destructive?

Do you ever tend to put your straps on others because they've worked for you? Do you ever look at others' Christian walks and think if they did certain things that they would be better off? If so, which things?

Do you believe that God feels the same way toward you when you sin as He felt toward Jesus when He did not sin? Discuss your thoughts on this.

If Jesus has saved you, nothing can separate you from Him. There is no way you will ever be dropped. Do you believe this? If so, how does this change how you live your life?

PART TWO

SET FREE *FROM*

For freedom Christ has set us free.

Galatians 5:1

The way we perceive and understand the world around us is skewed by what we already know or think we know. We just can't help it. Our preconceptions affect our work, our relationships, even our view of color. My daughter shared a fascinating study from her sociology class with our family over dinner recently. Apparently, some cultures have no word that differentiates green from blue.[1] If you show people from those cultures a bunch of green squares and one blue square, they will have a hard time finding the blue one.

They *literally* cannot see it.

Seriously. My mind was blown.

This phenomenon helps explain why we have a hard time understanding our freedom in Christ. It is as if our brains have *literally* been programmed by sin and the world around us to think differently about freedom than what the Bible tells us it is.

In this section of the book, we are going to dive into the Bible and let it answer this question for us: What has Jesus set us free *from?*

CHAPTER 3

SET FREE *FROM THE LAW*

I don't scare easily, but one thing in particular gets my blood pumping and my heart racing in fear: teaching my teenagers to drive. I have been through it three times, and I have one more in the pipeline.

"You have to come to a complete stop!"

"The speed limit is thirty-five!"

"You can't enter the highway using the exit ramp!" (I actually had to say that once.)

During each of these brief seasons of perfectly reasonable terror, I found myself the biggest advocate for obeying the law. I often reminded my children that they were driving a "murder machine" and that, if they broke the law, great penalties would await them, ranging from increased insurance rates, prison, or even death.

Eventually my campaign of terror would come to an end on the day they were back in the passenger seat and I was back to the safety of the driver's seat. Armed with their newfound knowledge and experience came a new sense of responsibility … to tell me how well I was driving.

"You have to come to a complete stop!"

"The speed limit is thirty-five!"

"You can't enter the highway using the exit ramp!" (No, they never said that; I'm not *that* bad of a driver.)

In those moments, a parent can go one of two directions. The first is to go old school and declare, "Do as I say, not as I do!" The second, which is the route I took, is to begin to explain when you can get away with breaking the law.

"It's a rolling stop. No one else is around."

"Thirty-nine is fine. You won't get pulled over until you go over forty."

The message I taught my kids was clear: "You can break the law as long as you don't get caught." It's a discipleship moment many parents (like me) fail, but it also raises a crucial theological question: What is a Christian's relationship with the Law?

Now, when I say "the Law," I'm not talking about laws like obeying speed limits and stop signs, but the Law we find in the Old Testament of the Bible (hence the big *L*). This is an important concept to wrestle with because the Law is one of the central themes of Scripture and is mentioned directly more than two hundred times and indirectly more times than I can count.

But first a warning.

The Law is one of those topics that gets so hotly debated in Christianity that we risk violating the command the apostle Paul gave Titus when he told him to "avoid foolish controversies, genealogies, dissensions, and quarrels about the law, for they are unprofitable and worthless" (Titus 3:9).

This doesn't mean discussing or studying the Law isn't important or even vital. We just need to be careful not to come to a point where healthy debate with fellow Christians turns into ungodly quarreling that detracts from the gospel. To honor this principle, I am going to do my best to clearly lay out my understanding of the Law as it relates to the gospel and our freedom in Christ without getting into every single nuance regarding the Law. Admittedly, this approach will leave some wanting. For a more comprehensive study on the various positions held by faithful followers of Jesus, I highly recommend the excellent work *Five Views on Law and Gospel*, edited by Stanley N. Gundry.[1] For more on the view I lean toward, check out *Law and Gospel* by William McDavid, Ethan Richardson, and David Zahl.[2] I've also included (in the appendix) a quick survey of every mention of the Law in the New Testament. That should get you started if this chapter doesn't scratch your Law itch.

WHAT IS THE LAW?

Simply put, the Law is a set of 613 specific rules God gave Israel (Lev. 26:46; Rom. 2:14; 9:4) in the Old Testament of the Bible. Of that total, 248 are positive (do these things) and 365 are negative (don't do these things). These laws help us know what God cares about and what sin is (Gal. 3:19–25), and they are commonly broken down into three categories:

- The Moral Law—how the Jews were to determine right and wrong
- The Civil Law—how they were to interact with each other and the people around them
- The Ceremonial Law—how Israel was to worship God

These three little categories are fairly helpful when studying the Law, but they are also where we can get easily spun around. They fall on the "useful scale," somewhere between chapter and verse designations (which were added to help people efficiently find the same section of Scripture) and systematic theologies (that help us logically process our faith). They cease to be helpful when they cause us to treat some of the Law as *really* important, other parts as *kind of* important, and still other parts as *quaint* and *irrelevant*.

But that's how we like to treat all laws, isn't it?

Embezzling a billion dollars doesn't feel quite the same as absconding with a ream of paper from the office, right? Sure, they are both technically stealing, but come on! Is a couple of bucks worth of paper that big a deal?

This attitude bleeds into how we view the Law. We tend to treat some of it (such as the Ten Commandments) as a big deal and other parts (such as the dietary restriction not to eat shellfish) with less value. And even within the Ten Commandments we like to pick and choose! As a reminder, here's the "Big 10":

1. You shall have no other gods before me.

2. You shall not make for yourself a carved image, or any likeness of anything that is in heaven above, or that is on the earth beneath, or that is in the water under the earth.

3. You shall not take the name of the LORD your God in vain, for the LORD will not hold him guiltless who takes his name in vain.

4. Remember the Sabbath day, to keep it holy.

5. Honor your father and your mother, that your days may be long in the land that the LORD your God is giving you.

6. You shall not murder.

7. You shall not commit adultery.

8. You shall not steal.

9. You shall not bear false witness against your neighbor.

10. You shall not covet your neighbor's house; you shall not covet your neighbor's wife, or his male servant, or his female servant, or his ox, or his donkey, or anything that is your neighbor's. (Exod. 20:3–17)

Don't some of these seem far more important than others? Surely if you were doing a ranking, "Do not murder" would sit at a higher level than "Do not covet your neighbor's donkey." And

"Honor your father and mother"? Are you telling me that's up there with "Do not steal"?

While we're at it, what's up with the Sabbath? When was the last time (be honest, because lying is number nine on the list) you *really* kept the Sabbath?

That means no work on Saturday.

None.

I will even allow you to consider Sunday your Sabbath if you want to think of it that way. When was the last time you took the *whole day Sunday* and set it apart for God? No checking your work email. No mowing the lawn. No work. Nada.

Before you answer, take a minute to consider how big of a deal the Sabbath is to God:

> You are to speak to the people of Israel and say, "Above all you shall keep my Sabbaths, for this is a sign between me and you throughout your generations, that you may know that I, the LORD, sanctify you. You shall keep the Sabbath, because it is holy for you." (Exod. 31:13–14)

"Above all you shall keep my Sabbaths." *Above all!* That's a big deal! In fact, if you feel like some parts of the Law are more important than others, you better rank this one right at the top. Honoring the Sabbath is such a big deal that breaking it comes with a monster consequence:

> Everyone who profanes [the Sabbath] *shall be*
> *put to death*. Whoever does any work on it, that
> soul shall be cut off from among his people. Six
> days shall work be done, but the seventh day
> is a Sabbath of solemn rest, holy to the LORD.
> Whoever does any work on the Sabbath day *shall*
> *be put to death*. (Exod. 31:14–15)

Death.

The consequence for breaking the Sabbath is death.

Okay, now you can answer, when was the last time you kept the Sabbath?

This is terrifying stuff, isn't it? That's why we have to be careful when we are dealing with the Law. We have to get this right! It was so important to the Israelites that their entire world circled around it. God commanded them in this way:

> And these words that I command you today shall
> be on your heart. You shall teach them diligently
> to your children, and shall talk of them when you
> sit in your house, and when you walk by the way,
> and when you lie down, and when you rise. You
> shall bind them as a sign on your hand, and they
> shall be as frontlets between your eyes. You shall
> write them on the doorposts of your house and
> on your gates. (Deut. 6:6–9)

The Law (every single bit of it) was integrated into their entire lives. You could even say that it *was* their entire lives.

Now, even though the Law was given to the Jews and it directly applied to them alone, Paul makes an interesting observation for those of us who are not Jewish:

> For when Gentiles, who do not have the law, by nature do what the law requires, they are a law to themselves, even though they do not have the law. They show that the work of the law is written on their hearts, while their conscience also bears witness, and their conflicting thoughts accuse or even excuse them. (Rom. 2:14–15)

The Law is written on every human heart. It doesn't matter if you are a Jew, a Gentile, a senior citizen, a teenager, a toddler, a Democrat, or Kim Jong Un, the Law is etched into the core of your being. All of us have a conscience that tells us about the Law, and that means our (often conflicting) thoughts battle daily over what is right and wrong. Sometimes our conscience excuses us—sometimes it accuses us. But that doesn't mean every person naturally understands the Law or what it means for them. Paul tells us our consciences can be damaged (1 Tim. 1:19; 4:2) and our thoughts can be tainted with sin (Mark 8:33; Acts 14:2; Rom. 1:28), but nevertheless, deep down every one of us knows what the Law requires; it is written on our hearts.

When my daughter Emma was just a bit over four years old, we moved into a new house. As any new home owner does, we did some redecorating, complete with a fresh coat of paint. Emma, clearly inspired by her dad's fantastic painting skills, decided to do some artwork of her own. She drew a cute little house, a tree, and a few stick figures on her canvas, which happened to be our freshly painted living room wall.

When her mother and I saw the masterpiece, we were less than impressed. We asked her, "Did you draw this?" Without missing a beat, the little sinner said, "No, Jesse did." Now, either her one-and-a-half-year-old brother was an artistic prodigy or Emma was a bald-faced liar.

Eventually, the truth came out.

Why did she lie? We had never, to my recollection, told her not to write on the wall. It had never crossed our minds that we needed to. But, even without our explicit instructions, she knew it was wrong and she was afraid.

That's what the Law being written on our hearts does; it shows the distance between our behavior and God's standard. Even as four-year-olds, we sense that something is cosmically wrong with our lives. And because of that gap, we go into defense mode whenever someone tells us how we "ought to" behave.

Consider it this way: what's the first word you think of when you hear the word *Law*?

Judgment?

Punishment?

Restrictions?

Laying down the Law? (I know that's four words. I'm a law breaker.)

Generally, we are not fans of the Law. Don't get me wrong—we are fine with the laws we want to obey, but we dislike those we want to break and those we think are unworthy of our obedience. It's not hard for any of us to come up with laws that fall into this latter category, and most of them are traffic related. And if we don't like being told to keep our car's speed to fifty-five miles per hour, how much more disdain do we naturally have for God's Law, especially the stuff that seems silly to us?

For example, most of us can get behind "You shall not murder" (Exod. 20:13). But when God says, "You shall not wear a garment of cloth made of two kinds of material" (see Lev. 19:19), we say, "I don't want to obey that because it's stupid—and my favorite shirt is a wrinkle-free cotton-poly blend."

Unfortunately for our Law-breaking hearts, we don't have the luxury of making the distinction! Listen to what God has to say about the Law (the whole thing): "So the law is holy, and the commandment is holy and righteous and good" (Rom. 7:12; see also Rom. 7:16; 1 Tim. 1:8).

Listen to those adjectives: "Holy!" "Righteous!" "Good!" That's what the Law is … every little bit of it!

THE MOST IMPORTANT LAW

The religious leaders of Jesus's day knew the whole Law was equally binding, so they tried to trap Jesus by asking Him which was the most important part. It was a brilliant strategy. If He refused to answer, He would look weak. If He ranked any part of the Law over another, they could play "gotcha" by trying to catch Him in a debate between different teachers who emphasized different portions. So what did Jesus do? He gave them an answer that boiled the Law down to its essence and gave the entire thing a singular focus.

> You shall love the Lord your God with all your heart and with all your soul and with all your mind. This is the great and first commandment. And a second is like it: You shall love your neighbor as yourself. On these two commandments depend all the Law and the Prophets. (Matt. 22:37–40)

Jesus's answer was masterful. He reminded them what we intuitively know: while the whole Law was equally important and binding, parts of it are *weightier*. He even flat-out said as much in the next chapter (Matt. 23:23). He was reminding them that the whole Law (all 613 bits of it) swirled around a central theme: love God, and love people. Quoting from two different sections of the Law (Deut. 6:5; Lev. 19:18), Jesus brought them together to create a focal point, a singular emphasis: love. Paul followed His lead when he said love was not only the summary of the Law but also the fulfillment of the Law (Gal. 5:14). James went so far as to refer to love as "the royal law" (James 2:8). While we tend to think "commandment" when we consider the Law, Jesus thinks "love."

THE "IF" FACTOR

Scripture also comes with a warning that we better take as seriously as we take the Law itself:

> Now we know that the law is good, if one uses it lawfully, understanding this, that the law is not laid down for the just but for the lawless and disobedient, for the ungodly and sinners, for the unholy and profane, for those who strike their fathers and mothers, for murderers, the sexually immoral, men who practice homosexuality, enslavers, liars, perjurers, and whatever else is contrary to sound doctrine. (1 Tim. 1:8–10)

"The Law is good *if* …"

"If" is an essential word to understanding and applying the Law.

"If" tells me there is a wrong way of using the Law, one that moves it from "good" to "ungood." It is possible to take the good Law and make something bad out of it. How? Well, what did Paul say? The Law is not to be laid down for whom?

The just.

Is "the just" someone who keeps the Law perfectly? It can't be! If that were the case, Jesus would be the only person to qualify. Who was Paul talking about? He was talking about someone who had been *made perfect* by Jesus. In other words, if you are "in Christ" (Rom. 3:24; 6:23; 8:1; 1 Cor. 1:30; 2 Cor. 5:17), if you have been saved by grace through faith (Rom. 4:16; 5:2; Eph. 2:8), you are the just (Rom. 5:1, 9; 8:30–33; 1 Cor. 6:11), and *the Law is not laid down for you* (Gal. 3:10, 12; 5:3; James 2:10; 1 Tim. 1:8–11). The Law exists to shine a light on your sin in order to drive you to Jesus. Once you are safe and secure in Him, it has completed its purpose. It's notable that Paul's entire rant regarding the Law was directed specifically toward those who wanted "to be teachers of the law, without understanding either what they are saying or the things about which they make confident assertions" (1 Tim. 1:7). In other words, they were trying to apply the Law to those Jesus had already saved.

You see, the Law had its time. It served a significant purpose as a "guardian" (Gal. 3:24) and something that "held [us] captive" (Gal. 3:23) until Jesus came. When He came, He perfectly fulfilled the Law and its demands by living a sinless life. His death, burial, and resurrection put a period on the end of the Law's sentence.

WHAT GOOD IS THE LAW NOW?

Can we just ignore the Law or carry around only New Testaments, never to look at the Old Testament again? No! The Law still has great use for those of us who are not under it, showing us we are sinners who need to be saved. It reminds us we are hopeless and helpless. You can't help but read the Law and have a growing pit in your stomach when you see how different you are from God. Sin is any failure to reflect the image of God in nature, attitude, and action, and the Law shows us how we fail in all three. In that sense, the Law fulfills its ultimate purpose: *it serves as a giant arrow pointing at Jesus.*

Oh, and I get this idea from Jesus Himself. Listen to what He had to say about the Law:

> Do not think that I have come to abolish the Law
> or the Prophets; I have not come to abolish them
> but to fulfill them. For truly, I say to you, until
> heaven and earth pass away, not an iota, not a
> dot, will pass from the Law until all is accom-
> plished. (Matt. 5:17–18)

Jesus is the fulfillment of the Law (Luke 24:44; John 1:45; 12:34; Rom. 3:21, 31; 8:4; Gal. 3:13). How did He do it? By accomplishing it all! By fulfilling it all! But wait, Paul seemed to say the opposite of what Jesus said:

> But now in Christ Jesus you who once were
> far off have been brought near by the blood of
> Christ. For he himself is our peace, who has made
> us both one and has broken down in his flesh the
> dividing wall of hostility by *abolishing the law* of
> commandments expressed in ordinances, that he
> might create in himself one new man in place of
> the two, so making peace. (Eph. 2:13–15)

Jesus fulfilled the Law, accomplishing all that it required. In doing so, He abolished the binding power of the Law while not abolishing its purpose, which, again, He fulfilled. That's why Paul could go on to say, *"For Christ is the end of the law for righteousness to everyone who believes"* (Rom. 10:4).

Paul was repeatedly accused of being "anti-Law" (see Acts 18:13; 21:28) because he proclaimed all the stuff we just covered. So what was his response to his critics? In Acts 21–25, he used the Law again and again and again (because it is useful) to point people to Jesus. But the reason Paul kept getting accused of being anti-Law was one simple reason: he refused to climb back under the Law he had been set free from, with one very notable exception.

When Paul was trying to tell people who were "under the Law" about Jesus, he placed himself back under it. Why? To love them, which is the very point of the Law in the first place!

> For though I am free from all, I have made myself
> a servant to all, that I might win more of them. To

the Jews I became as a Jew, in order to win Jews. To those under the law I became as one under the law (though not being myself under the law) that I might win those under the law. To those outside the law I became as one outside the law (not being outside the law of God but under the law of Christ) that I might win those outside the law. To the weak I became weak, that I might win the weak. I have become all things to all people, that by all means I might save some. I do it all for the sake of the gospel, that I may share with them in its blessings. (1 Cor. 9:19–23)

Paul used the Law to point people to Jesus, and he even placed himself under its demands, not because he was under the Law, but rather to gain a hearing with Jews. We are going to get into this a lot more in chapter 9, but for now, look at these examples of how he used the Law—and, more importantly, how he didn't use it:

By [Jesus] everyone who believes is freed from everything from which you could not be freed by the law of Moses. (Acts 13:39)

Yet we know that a person is not justified by works of the law but through faith in Jesus Christ, so we also have believed in Christ Jesus, in order to be justified by faith in Christ and not by works of the law, because by works of the law no one will be justified. (Gal. 2:16; see also Rom. 3:28; Gal. 3:11)

For sin will have no dominion over you, since you are not under law but under grace. (Rom. 6:14)

What was Paul saying? To summarize:

- If you believe in Jesus, you are free (something the Law couldn't do).
- You are justified by faith in Jesus (not by trying to obey the Law).
- Because you are under grace, sin won't rule over you (as it did when you were under the Law).

This last one is the sticky point for many, many people. They think that if a Christian is not under the Law, he will abuse his freedom and use it as an excuse to do whatever he wants to do. Paul said, essentially, "That's not how this grace thing works." It is precisely *because* you are free from the Law that you are set free not to sin (a fact we will cover a lot more in chapter 5). In fact, as I am sitting here typing this, I am having a hard time coming up with a single example of someone I have met who has used freedom from the Law as an excuse to do something explicitly sinful. It actually works the opposite way. When you genuinely begin to grasp the freedom Jesus offers and the enormity of God's love in procuring it for you, you gradually see sin for what it is: the enemy.

So now what? Is there a law for a follower of Jesus to follow? Yes! We, as followers of Jesus, now live under a new law. The old Law was about "have to" and "fear" and "bondage." The new law is about "want to" and "love" and "freedom." This new law is given four names in the New Testament: "the law of Christ," "the law of faith," "the law of the Spirit of life," and "the law of liberty."

THE LAW OF CHRIST

Remember, now that we have been set free (brought outside of the box we talked about in chapter 1), we are *positionally* with Jesus. He is the period at the end of the sentence; so it's appropriate that this new law is named after him. Here's how Paul laid it out in the passage we already looked at:

> To those outside the law I became as one outside the law (not being outside the law of God but under the law of Christ) that I might win those outside the law. (1 Cor. 9:21)

How fantastic is this! Paul boldly declared, "I am not under the law" *and* "I am not outside the law." Instead, he found he was "under the law of Christ." And where does this new law have its focus?

Loving God and loving others.

These were precisely the focal points of the entire Mosaic Law, but they have found their ultimate expression in the gospel of Jesus. Paul's motivation in life was no longer one of fear or dread or obligation; instead, it was one of love and gratitude and the desire to see others share in what he had found by placing his faith in Jesus. In fact, that's another name for this new law: the law of faith.

THE LAW OF FAITH

(Read also Rom. 4:14; Gal. 3:10–14.)

Paul, when challenged by those who bragged that they kept the Law and it saved them, said this: "Then what becomes of our boasting? It is excluded. By what kind of law? By a law of works? No, but by the law of faith. *For we hold that one is justified by faith apart from works of the law*" (Rom. 3:27–28).

If we could participate at all in our salvation (by doing the right stuff or not doing the wrong stuff), then we would certainly figure out a way to brag about it. But since we can't, we don't, which is a good thing because that would "nullify the grace of God, for if righteousness were through the law, then Christ died for no purpose" (Gal. 2:21; see also Rom. 4:14; Heb. 7:11). No one can be made righteous through obedience to the Law. If they could, Jesus's death was in vain.

As a follower of Jesus, when you try to take credit for anything good you have done in your life, you miss the point. You can't save you. You were saved by Jesus, and then God went to work on you to conform you into Jesus's image through the power of the Holy Spirit (Rom. 8:28–29). Stop trying to pull yourself up by your bootstraps, and instead put your focus on Him! He is at work in your life. In fact, that's the next name of this new law.

THE LAW OF THE SPIRIT OF LIFE

(Read also Gal. 5:18.)

One of the most astonishing chunks of Scripture is found in Romans 8, where Paul wrote:

> There is therefore now no condemnation for those who are in Christ Jesus. For the law of the Spirit of life has set you free in Christ Jesus from the law of sin and death. For God has done what the law, weakened by the flesh, could not do. By sending his own Son in the likeness of sinful flesh and for sin, he condemned sin in the flesh, in order that the righteous requirement of the law might be fulfilled in us, who walk not according to the flesh but according to the Spirit. For those who live according to the flesh set their minds on the things of the flesh, but those who live according to the Spirit set their minds on the things of the Spirit. For to set the mind on the flesh is death, but to set the mind on the Spirit is life and peace. For the mind that is set on the flesh

is hostile to God, for it does not submit to God's
law; indeed, it cannot. Those who are in the flesh
cannot please God.

You, however, are not in the flesh but in the
Spirit, if in fact the Spirit of God dwells in you.
(vv. 1–9)

Do you get how astounding this is? Look at it backward: "If
in fact the Spirit of God dwells in you … you are *not condemned.*"

How can you know? Because you are set free in Christ!

The Law couldn't do it because your flesh and my flesh are
weakened.

That's precisely why Jesus came: He came to handle sin. He
condemned sin by taking it on Himself on the cross, and every
single requirement of the Law was handled!

You know what all of this means?

There is nothing left to be done. You can now live free.

Look at this again:

For those who live according to the flesh set their
minds on the things of the flesh, but those who
live according to the Spirit set their minds on the
things of the Spirit. For to set the mind on the
flesh is death, but to set the mind on the Spirit
is life and peace. For the mind that is set on the
flesh is hostile to God, for it does not submit to
God's law; indeed, it cannot. (vv. 5–7)

What is the Law good for? Telling our flesh that it is sinful. And when we set our minds on what we can do in our flesh, it is nothing but death.

Remember the box? We, as followers of Jesus, lift our eyes from the box (filled with our sinfulness), raise them to the Spirit, and say, "Okay, I trust You with this. I trust that through You I can live in the freedom of being outside this wretched box." I don't know about you, but that is a freedom I long for. Maybe that's why this new law has one final name (with an ironic twist).

THE LAW OF LIBERTY

(Read also Gal. 2:4; 5:1, 13; 1 Pet. 2:16; 2 Pet. 2:19.)

> Therefore put away all filthiness and rampant wickedness and receive with meekness the implanted word, which is able to save your souls.
>
> But be doers of the word, and not hearers only, deceiving yourselves. For if anyone is a hearer of the word and not a doer, he is like a man who looks intently at his natural face in a mirror. For he looks at himself and goes away and at once forgets what he was like. But the one who looks into the perfect law, the law of liberty, and perseveres, being no hearer who forgets but a doer who acts, he will be blessed in his doing. (James 1:21–25)

The image James is trying to paint is of someone who doesn't know how to use a mirror, is stupid, or both. This guy looked intently at himself and immediately forgot what he looked like when he turned the other direction. In context, it's obvious this guy is not correcting some obvious flaw he sees like a hair out of place or a crooked tie.

Who would be so stupid?

Apparently, I would.

One morning years ago, I got dressed and looked at myself in the mirror. Much to my surprise, the sweater I was wearing wasn't a V-neck like I remembered it was. I didn't think too much about it, but each time I passed a mirror the entire day, I would think in passing, *That is so weird!*

When I came home after a full day at work (complete with meetings and interactions with a lot of people), my wife greeted me with an affectionate "You dork!"

"What?"

"You're wearing your sweater backward! Have you looked that stupid all day? Didn't you look at a mirror? And if you did, why didn't you fix it?"

James reminds us that so many people treat the Word of God the way I treated the mirror that day. It had some pretty good information for me, but I didn't give it enough consideration. Instead of merely glancing at God's Word, James challenges his readers to look intently into the *law of liberty* and consider the changes it makes in their lives.

You know what happens when you live smack-dab in the law of liberty? You end up obeying God. You love God and you love people. Why? Not because you are fearful or because God is keeping some kind of tabs on you. You love God and you love people because God loved you and saved you in Jesus. You do good things not because they will save you but because Jesus has already saved you. You begin to see all the commands in the New Testament (and there are hundreds of them, both the "do this" and the "don't do this" types of commands) not as burdens but as joys because God is busy reorienting your affections toward Him and His priorities.

When we looked into the old Law, all we saw was condemnation. Now, staring into "the perfect law, the law of liberty," we see Jesus, who has set us free, and we want to emulate Him. His humility (Phil. 2:8)—even though He is God—causes us to see ourselves in a humbler light. His joyful suffering (Heb. 12:2) helps us make it through a difficult marriage. His courageousness when faced with those who opposed God and His Word (John 18:19–23) inspires us to be the same.

The more you live in the law of liberty, the more you find yourself filtering your actions through the big question that governed Jesus's life: Does this love God and love people? And you let God, instead of the world around you, define love.

SO WHAT IS A CHRISTIAN'S RELATIONSHIP WITH THE LAW?

I was reading an article[3] online, and I love what the authors said. Simply, they said, it was like God gave the Jews the rules for soccer and Jesus changed the game to a team marathon. He took away the first rule book and handed us a new one. Both sports have some basics in common (being healthy and being able to run). Both require devotion to the coach and the team. But the rules are different for each. Soccer has a lot more rules than a marathon, and the scoring is totally different. In fact, that's where the big difference is. As followers of Jesus, we aren't trying to rack up as many points as we can to "win." We run for the joy of running, knowing Jesus ran the race so well that He already won for our whole team.

DISCUSSION QUESTIONS

What is your understanding of the Law? Do you take some parts of it more seriously than others? Or is it something you don't think about much at all?

Are you naturally more of a Law follower or a Law breaker? Why do you think that is?

According to Romans 2, the Law is written on every human heart. How have you seen evidence of this in your own life or in the lives of those around you?

What is the first word that comes to mind when you hear the word "Law"? Why do you think that is? Discuss your experiences with the Law.

Talk about why we tend to think "commandment" when we consider the Law but Jesus thinks "love." What does this tell us about ourselves? What does it tell us about Jesus?

The Law exists to show us our sin and drive us to Jesus, and once we are in Him, it's done serving its purpose. If this is true, why do so many Christians still insist on holding on to parts of the Law?

Jesus "abolished the binding power of the Law while not abolishing its purpose, which He fulfilled." What is the difference between abolishing the binding power of the Law but not its purpose?

Being set free from the Law frees us *not* to sin, and it actually helps us much more than if we were still under the Law. If a Christian really believes he isn't under the Law, might he abuse this grace and just do whatever he wants? Have you ever personally seen this play out in someone's life?

The new law we are under is about love and freedom rather than fear and bondage. Are most Christians you know characterized by fear and freedom (old Law) or by love and freedom (new law)?

Review the different names for the new law. Then discuss the questions for each of those names.

> **The law of Christ:** "Paul's motivation in life was no
> longer one of fear or dread or obligation; instead,

it was one of love and gratitude and desire to see others share in what he had found by placing his faith in Jesus." Would you say your motivation in life is more often one of fear, dread, and obligation, or one of love, gratitude, and desire?

The law of faith: We are justified by our faith in Christ, not by anything we do or don't do. What are some practical ways believers can put their focus on Jesus and faith in Him instead of trying to do more to gain His approval?

The law of the Spirit of life: What does it look like to set your mind on the things of the flesh? What does it look like to set your mind on the things of the Spirit? Have you ever experienced life and peace from setting your mind on the Spirit rather than on the flesh? What did this look like for you?

The law of liberty: How has the love God has for you changed how you love God or people? Have you stared into "the perfect law, the law of liberty" long enough to see how much Jesus has set you free from? Has looking intently into Him ever caused you to walk away from sin and emulate Him?

Everything we do should be filtered through the same question that Jesus used as His filter: Does this love God and love people? What are some things in your life that might change if you filtered them through this question? How would the Christian church as a whole change if we were to do this?

CHAPTER 4

SET FREE *FROM* RELIGION

"Christianity isn't a religion! It's a relationship!"

Ever heard that one?

Not only have I heard it, but I've also said it—many times. In fact, when I was in my twenties, I took part in a summer project that did evangelism on a beach in South Carolina, and we were required to use gospel tracts, simple little pamphlets that explain the gospel in a few minutes. In the 1970s and 1980s, these booklets were all the rage, and I know a number of people who became Christians because someone shared one with them. By the time the 1990s hit, tracts had mostly gone the way of VHS tapes and parachute pants, but I was connected with one of the few groups that still swore by them.

I wasn't generally a fan of tracts, and I really didn't like the outdated ones I was given, so before heading to the beach, I made my own. Right across the tiny little cover were the words in big, bold, uppercase letters stating my very blunt opinion of religion.

I really do think I had the right motives in creating these tracts. My desire was to defend Christianity passionately from the gross mischaracterization that it was just like every other religion out there. But I'm not sure I was right to throw religion under the bus—at least not completely.

You see, one of the most counterintuitive notions behind Jesus setting us free is that He launched a new religion in the process and that this new religion sets us free from, well, religion.

Stick with me here.

To work our way through this, we have to start by defining the word *religion* so we know what we are talking about. And because we are dealing with most people's *perceptions* of the word, it would seem appropriate to use a definition most people would generally agree with. Let's call religion "what you believe and the practices that come with those beliefs." Now, if that's what most people think (and from my experience, it is), then common sense would make any casual observer say that, yes, Christianity is a religion. So it's no surprise that it comes across as fairly incongruous to our nonbelieving friends when we keep asserting that Christianity is not a religion. In fact, the Bible itself would agree with them, and it's actually pretty easy to check this because the word *religion* appears in only three biblical contexts.

The first was when a Roman official named Festus was trying to sort out why the Jews and Paul were at odds with each other. His description of the events was pretty straightforward: "[The

Jews] had certain points of dispute with [Paul] about their own religion and about a certain Jesus, who was dead, but whom Paul asserted to be alive" (Acts 25:19). It is encouraging to see that the thing that was getting Paul in trouble was his insistence on the resurrection of Jesus. This belief is at the core of the Christian faith, and Festus concluded that the case in front of him was essentially a theological debate between some religious guys. Not knowing the nuances, he lumped Judaism and Christianity together and called their collective belief system a "religion." At this point, we can see that *religion* is a rather neutral biblical term, with neither positive nor negative connotations.

A chapter later, Paul used the word when defending himself in the very same dispute:

> My manner of life from my youth, spent from the beginning among my own nation and in Jerusalem, is known by all the Jews. They have known for a long time, if they are willing to testify, that according to the strictest party of our religion I have lived as a Pharisee. (Acts 26:4–5)

Here Paul declared himself to be (or to have been) a part of the religion of Judaism. In fact, Paul saw Christianity as the logical next step of the Jewish faith, kind of like a Judaism 2.0. Because the Jews were anxiously awaiting the long-promised Messiah and Jesus was the one they had been waiting for, it made sense for this to be the continuation of their faith. Again, the biblical use of the term *religion* is neutral; it's merely a word that describes a belief system. It's only when you stick an unspoken adjective on the front of the word that it carries any moral weight: "self-made religion," "man-made religion," or "grace-based religion."

It would be difficult to make a case at this point that *religion*, in and of itself, is a bad thing. The Bible, so far, seems to agree.

In Colossians, Paul used the word again, this time to contrast true, biblical Christianity with a different *type* of religion:

> If with Christ you died to the elemental spirits of the world, why, as if you were still alive in the world, do you submit to regulations—"Do not handle, do not taste, do not touch" (referring to things that all perish as they are used)—according to human precepts and teachings? These have indeed an appearance of wisdom in promoting *self-made religion* and asceticism and severity to the body, but they are of no value in stopping the indulgence of the flesh. (2:20–23)

Now we begin to see the crucial difference we have been getting at this entire book and, quite frankly, why *religion* receives such a bad rap. Christianity is not a "self-made religion" full of all kinds of *dos and don'ts*.

Paul is clear that this type of religion doesn't work; it has no value. In his short explanation, he helps us understand why this sort of religion is so attractive. It would appear that people are searching for a way to "[stop] the indulgence of the flesh." In other words, because the Law is written on everyone's hearts, because we are all created in the image of God, we know (no matter how much that knowledge is buried) that there is a way we *should* live and that we aren't doing it. So we create systems of belief and behavior (you could say "self-made religions") to help us out. These attempts to reconcile us with God (or the universe or just each other) come by way of "asceticism and severity to the body."

What does that mean?

Asceticism means to deny yourself of something, and "severity to the body" is taking that idea to the physical extreme. Paul describes this as the "do not handle, do not taste, do not touch" way of living.

Let's stop there.

If you were looking at Christianity from the outside, how would you describe it? Dare I say, "Do not handle, do not taste, do not touch"? We don't appear to be any different in the message we often proclaim.

That's why so many faithful followers of Jesus want to declare, "Christianity is not a religion!"

But it is. It's just a religion that has a different source: God. The fundamental difference is that it is not "human precepts and teachings." It's not a "do not handle, do not taste, do not touch" religion.

In James, we come across our last use of the word *religion*, and this one again contrasts a positive and negative religion:

> If anyone thinks he is religious and does not bridle his tongue but deceives his heart, this person's religion is worthless. Religion that is pure and undefiled before God the Father is this: to visit orphans and widows in their affliction, and to keep oneself unstained from the world. (1:26–27)

Okay, wait a minute. This looks like another list of *dos* and *don'ts*! Isn't that the same thing as those "do not handle, do not taste, do not touch" religions? Not at all! Look closely and you will see the heart of God reflected in these verses. What's at the core of bridling your tongue, visiting orphans, and taking care of widows? What does it mean to keep oneself unstained from the world?

Love.

That's the kind of life that God calls His people to.

Let's pull this all together. From a biblical perspective, *religion* is a neutral term, and while there is a kind of religion that is negative, there is another kind of religion that is pleasing to God. You could say that true religion is Jesus-focused, grace-based, love-centered religion.

SO WHY DO PEOPLE SAY, "IT'S NOT A RELIGION; IT'S A RELATIONSHIP"?

This has become a well-meaning but not altogether accurate phrase that tries to describe a critical distinction between Christianity and every other religion in the world. One of the earliest usages of this cliché I could find was in a publication of the Episcopal Church in 1958. That article says:

> May we go forward remembering that Christianity is not a religion which merely lays upon us weak, human beings the hopeless task of living an impossibly good life helped only by the example of a man who lived a perfect human life 2,000 years ago, but rather that Christianity is a relationship to God whereby He communicates to us His strength and vitality which enables us to live on a higher plane.[1]

That's not bad.

You see, every religion in the world—with the exception of Christianity—has at its core "human precepts and teachings." It is created by humans as a way to get to God. It is centered on humans, and therefore, it is fundamentally inside the box.

In the previous chapter, we saw how Jesus has set us free from the Law (which was God's holy law given to His people). Now we see that Jesus has set us free from religion (which is "holy law" given to people by people).

You can understand this most clearly when you set Christianity next to other major world religions. Every day, around the world, people practice religions that declare there is something they must *do* to appease God or the gods or to be right with the universe. Picture a ladder that is so tall it disappears into the stratosphere on a clear day. At the top of that ladder is God. Religion says, simply, "Climb."

For instance, Hinduism, at its most fundamental level, says that your actions during this life will determine how sweet your life will be the next time around and that this process continues again and again. This is, in a lot of ways, why people of a lower caste system are often looked down on—it is their fault (or their past lives' fault) that they are lower down on the societal ladder.

Buddhists have a similar belief in repeated rebirths that ultimately culminate in one that is filled with suffering. The only way to break free from this downward spiral is to stop all sensual pleasures and desires and empty yourself.

Islam has five essential actions all Muslims must perform: pledge a statement of allegiance to Allah (God) and the prophet Muhammad, pray five daily prayers, give based on your wealth, fast regularly, and go on a pilgrimage to Mecca, which must be performed once in your life.

Do you see the ladder?

Every single one of these religions says, "Do these things and you will (or may) be made right with God (or the universe)."

Christianity declares the opposite!

There is nothing at all for us to do because Jesus has already done everything for us (1 Pet. 2:24). You could say the ladder we climb has one rung and it looks like a cross (1 Cor. 1:18). All we can do is cling to it! The apostle Paul takes great pains in Ephesians to remind us that we have not been saved by anything we have done:

> And you were dead in the trespasses and sins in which you once walked, following the course of this world, following the prince of the power of the air, the spirit that is now at work in the sons of disobedience—among whom we all once lived in the passions of our flesh, carrying out the desires of the body and the mind, and were by nature children of wrath, like the rest of mankind. (2:1–3)

We all start out our lives ... dead. In fact, it would seem that this says we were all once the "walking dead," which makes our lives like a zombie TV show in reverse. We start out as the dead, and then we are made alive. And if you are in Christ, there is no way you can be more alive!

How did that happen?

> But God, being rich in mercy, because of the great love with which he loved us, even when we were dead in our trespasses, made us alive together with Christ—by grace you have been saved—and raised us up with him and seated us with him in the heavenly places in Christ Jesus, so that in the coming ages he might show the immeasurable riches of his grace in kindness toward us in Christ Jesus. (Eph. 2:4–7)

"But God." We are not left to our own devices. "But God." We often try to fix ourselves, pull ourselves up by our bootstraps. "But God." Many people think of God as far off and beyond our comprehension (which He is). But the amazing thing is that, even in His "bigness," we find Him "being rich in mercy, because of the great love with which he loved us, even when we were dead in our trespasses."

God is *rich in mercy*. Let that sink in. Don't think "rich" as in money. Think rich as in the richest, densest cake you have ever eaten. The first time I visited England, I was offered sticky-toffee pudding. My Midwestern American ears heard *stinky*-toffee pudding, and I was tempted to decline until I was strongly encouraged to give it a try. When it showed up, it looked like just a piece of chocolate cake with some sauce drizzled on it and a bit of whipped cream. What was all the fuss about?

Then I took a bite.

I'm not a dessert guy, but … Seriously.

It was so rich and deceptively decadent and … truly, I have no words.

That's how God is with mercy. He is so soaked in it that there are no words.

Mercy is not getting what we deserve, and with God, it's oozing everywhere. And when was God so rich in mercy? When we were choosing the path that took us away from Him. While we were His enemies, He was oozing mercy and love.

In chapter 1, I told the story of how I ran to the mission field as a college student partially to get away from my dad because of my failing grades, parking tickets, and credit-card debt. However, I didn't tell you what happened when I got home.

My dad took me to Pizza Hut.

You see, the whole time I was in Africa, I was craving a supreme pan pizza and I would write home telling my parents about this deep desire. So Dad took me to Pizza Hut.

On the short drive from the campus to the restaurant, I wondered how my dad was going to bring up my wasted freshman year and what my punishment was going to be. Sure, I was an adult, but Dad held the keys to my life. Literally, he held the keys to my car and was paying for my life. Was that all going to stop? I certainly deserved some sort of punishment. I was just hoping it wouldn't be too severe.

Each glorious bite of Pizza Hut supreme pan pizza came with a bitter aftertaste of trepidation. I kept waiting for the conversation to turn to my behavior.

But he didn't bring it up.

We talked about what classes I was taking, how I liked my new roommates—basic stuff like that. I began to wonder if, by some cosmic miracle, I had been handed a "get out of jail free" card.

We wrapped up our meal, Dad picked up the check, and we headed out into the parking lot.

No way. I couldn't believe I was going to get away with this.

At least that's what I thought. Then Dad invited me to step into the back of his big conversion van that was well equipped with plush seats, track lighting, and most importantly, a table. When he opened the door, I saw that the table was covered with parking tickets, grade reports, and credit-card statements.

I remember thinking, *I am never getting out of this van alive. I'm very glad my last meal was a Pizza Hut supreme pan pizza.*

I took a seat, and Dad fanned the mountain of paper across the table. He asked me to explain myself, which I tried to do while holding back my tears and a fair amount of full body tremors. I really had no good excuses, and I was prepared for the worst.

When I was finished talking, he paused, took a deep breath, and slid *all the papers* into a grocery bag. Not one was left. As I stared at where the record of my sin used to be, I couldn't for the life of me imagine why he needed the table clear. Was that where he was going to lay my dead body? Or maybe it wasn't so sinister;

maybe this was just the first of many conversations we were going to have about this over the coming days.

But then he spoke. And I will never forget the words that exuded the mercy of God. He said, simply, "This is the past. Don't do it again."

That's all.

The papers were swept away, and in one fell swoop my father had cleared away my sin that separated us and had restored our relationship.

I have not seen those papers since.

To this day, that moment remains one of the best pictures of the gospel I have ever experienced. This is what God did for us through Jesus. *Rich in mercy and love*, He doesn't give us what we deserve. In fact, Jesus once proclaimed something that sounded an awful lot like what my dad said: "Go and sin no more" (John 8:11 NLT).

The gospel boldly declares that God has changed everything by making us *alive* together with Christ! We started dead and moved to life "together with Christ." But that's not all. We get even more than mercy. We get grace: "By grace you have been saved."

While mercy is not getting what we deserve, grace is getting what we don't deserve. We don't deserve salvation!

Because God loved us and made us alive and poured out His grace on us, we have been moved out of the box. We skipped over the ladder, and He "raised us up with him and seated us with him in the heavenly places in Christ Jesus."

We are raised up (not just from death to life) but also to where Jesus is. We are right now with Jesus. We are seated with Him. And He is seated at the right hand of God the Father in the heavenly places. And God did this for a reason—a reason that sounds absolutely crazy. His position was "that in the coming ages he might show the immeasurable riches of his grace in kindness toward us in Christ Jesus."

We are saved so that in the next life God might pour out on us immeasurable portions of stuff we don't deserve. And just in case we missed the point, Paul gets out his hammer and starts beating the nail in.

> For by grace you have been saved through faith. And this is not your own doing; it is the gift of God, not a result of works, so that no one may boast. (Eph. 2:8–9)

You have been saved *by grace* (we already covered that) and the way that grace saves us is *through faith*.

What is faith?

> Now faith is the assurance of things hoped for, the conviction of things not seen. (Heb. 11:1)

Believing faith is that moment when it *clicks*: "Jesus is really God. Jesus really rose from the dead. Jesus really did it for me. I can't see Him. But I believe." And where do we get this faith? "This is not your own doing; it is the gift of God."

What isn't our own doing?

Being saved?

Grace?

Faith?

Yes! Even the faith that saves us is a gift from God. It's all Him. It's all a gift. If it weren't, what would we do with our salvation? We would boast of course! But since we had nothing to do with it, we can't. Every single aspect of our salvation is a free gift.

WHY I ACTUALLY MAY HAVE BEEN RIGHT ABOUT RELIGION (SORTA)

Well-meaning Christians, those with a desire to honor God and not cheapen the grace of God, inadvertently dishonor God and cheapen His grace by adding one rule after another to their lives in order to be "true Christians." The problem is when we add even a single ounce of human effort to the salvific recipe, as Paul noted, "a little leaven leavens the whole lump" (Gal. 5:9). Yes, he was talking about adding a single rule to our faith. And we don't stop there! We add rule after rule after rule, thinking our rituals and practices will make God happier with us than He would be if we did not practice them. We forget we are outside the box, and so we try to reconstruct a new ladder and a new self. In doing so, we go so far as to construct for ourselves a new man-made religion.

Let me put this as clearly as I can: Jesus has saved you—the Bible calls that "justification" (see Rom. 3:28). Jesus is saving you—the

Bible calls that "sanctification" (see John 17:18–19). Jesus will save you—the Bible calls that "glorification" (see Col. 3:4).

You aren't part of this equation at all except as the one who is in need of salvation. And once you are saved, you are not even responsible to keep yourself saved!

> What then shall we say to these things? If God is for us, who can be against us? He who did not spare his own Son but gave him up for us all, how will he not also with him graciously give us all things? Who shall bring any charge against God's elect? It is God who justifies. Who is to condemn? Christ Jesus is the one who died—more than that, who was raised—who is at the right hand of God, who indeed is interceding for us. Who shall separate us from the love of Christ? Shall tribulation, or distress, or persecution, or famine, or nakedness, or danger, or sword? As it is written,
>
> "For your sake we are being killed all the day long; we are regarded as sheep to be slaughtered."
>
> No, in all these things we are more than conquerors through him who loved us. For I am sure that neither death nor life, nor angels nor rulers, nor things present nor things to come,

> nor powers, nor height nor depth, nor anything
> else in all creation, will be able to separate us
> from the love of God in Christ Jesus our Lord.
> (Rom. 8:31–39)

But what about all those commands in the Bible? The "do this, don't do that" stuff? Are they important? Yes. But they are unrelated to our salvation, except in one way that we'll get to in chapter 8.

CHRISTIANITY ISN'T *JUST* A RELIGION; IT'S A RELATIONSHIP

When Jesus saves us, He does a remarkable thing. He enters into a relationship with us.

Perhaps this is why God goes to such great pains to use the best possible human-relationship metaphors to talk about our relationship with Him: we are His family and His friends.

FAMILY

One of the predominant themes in the Bible is that God's people are described as His kids. In the Old Testament, the Jews were called "the children of Israel" (Exod. 3:10). Countless times in the New Testament, the term "brother" (Acts 15:1, 3, 7; 1 Cor. 14:39) is used to describe Christians, and God Himself goes by the name "heavenly Father" (Matt. 6:26).

Unfortunately, this beautiful metaphor can become a bit clouded for a simple reason: our only point of reference for understanding family is in the box with us. Our parents, our siblings, our spouses, our in-laws—family can be messy in the box. We've seen marriages fall apart, siblings that don't talk for years, parents who exasperate their kids, and kids who hate them in return.

Additionally, our experiences end up coloring our understanding of God as our Father and Jesus as our big brother. That's why we need to let Scripture fill in the gaps for us, to help us think (and I have worked really hard not to use this phrase in this book) *outside the box.*

Here's the key to understanding our familial relationship with God: it is fundamentally an unequal relationship—because He is still God and we are still not. That's actually what makes the concept of being adopted into this family so amazing!

Jesus became fully human, and then on the cross He became all that is dirty and nasty about us (2 Cor. 5:21), not so we would stay in the nastiness, but so we would become like Him in His righteousness. He became like us so we would become like Him. In fact, the Bible says we are lifted up to where He is (Eph. 2:6)!

> For you did not receive the spirit of slavery to fall back into fear, but you have received the Spirit of adoption as sons, by whom we cry, "Abba! Father!" The Spirit himself bears witness with our spirit that we are children of God, and

if children, then heirs—heirs of God and fellow
heirs with Christ, provided we suffer with him
in order that we may also be glorified with him.
(Rom. 8:15–17)

Adoption is a beautiful gospel picture.

A couple in our church adopted a brother and sister from an orphanage in Mexico. Unfortunately, right when they were about to bring their children home, the two governments got involved and did what governments tend to do—royally messed things up. The entire adoption, which should have been smooth sailing, ground to a screeching halt. Their kids were trapped in Mexico and not just for a few weeks. It took years to get them home.

These lonely, vulnerable little children had parents they couldn't see. That's where our situation is the same as these two little kids'. We are trapped here, and our dad is somewhere else. There is a period of time between when we are adopted and when we are with our Father. So what do we do in the in between? How do we survive? Paul said, "The Spirit himself bears witness with our spirit that we are children of God."

God sent someone to be with us.

That's what my friends did. They hired someone to stay with their children. They sent a couple they trusted to live with their children in Mexico. Each and every day, this couple would tell the children about their parents and how much the parents longed to be with them. The couple would show them pictures and tell them stories. They would make their home with these orphan children, and their very presence would point them to the kids' adoptive parents.

This is what the Holy Spirit does in our lives. He takes up residence with us to remind us we are not alone and that one day we will be with our Father. Jesus said as much to His disciples when He declared:

> And I will ask the Father, and he will give you another Helper, to be with you forever, even the Spirit of truth, whom the world cannot receive, because it neither sees him nor knows him. You know him, for he dwells with you and will be in you.
>
> I will not leave you as orphans; I will come to you. (John 14:16–18)

Was it tough? You bet, but Paul says suffering is part of the process.

Our heavenly Father has sent the Holy Spirit to "bear witness with our spirit that we are children of God." He whispers and reminds us that our Dad loves us and longs to bring us home.

FRIENDS

Jesus had an odd set of friends, and they were the source of all sorts of insults and a bad reputation He picked up along the way. Here are Jesus's own words about Himself:

> The Son of Man has come eating and drinking,
> and you say, "Look at him! A glutton and a
> drunkard, a friend of tax collectors and sinners!"
> (Luke 7:34)

Just because of who He hung out with, Jesus's enemies accused Him of drinking too much, eating too much, and having some friends they didn't like. It's actually amazing who Jesus decides to be friends with—people like me. I'm sure His enemies would have had a field day if Jesus spent some time with me and my small group.

But we tend to have the same sort of problem with our "friend Jesus" as we have with our "brother Jesus," and that is we've never had someone in our lives quite like Him. Consequently, we define our relationship with Him based on our relationships with our other friends. Let's take a look at one passage of Scripture in which Jesus pretty clearly defines what being His friend is like and then think about our relationship with Him.

> This is my commandment, that you love one
> another as I have loved you. Greater love has no
> one than this, that someone lay down his life for
> his friends. *You are my friends if you do what I
> command you. No longer do I call you servants,
> for the servant does not know what his master is
> doing; but I have called you friends, for all that I
> have heard from my Father I have made known to*

you. You did not choose me, but I chose you and appointed you that you should go and bear fruit and that your fruit should abide, so that whatever you ask the Father in my name, he may give it to you. These things I command you, so that you will love one another.

If the world hates you, know that it has hated me before it hated you. If you were of the world, the world would love you as its own; but because you are not of the world, but I chose you out of the world, therefore the world hates you. Remember the word that I said to you: "A servant is not greater than his master." If they persecuted me, they will also persecute you. If they kept my word, they will also keep yours. But all these things they will do to you on account of my name, because they do not know him who sent me. (John 15:12–21)

Did you see the italicized part? Jesus says this about His friends:

Jesus's friends do what He commands them to do (which is "bear fruit," and it appears that fruit is love). This seems like a weird friendship, right? How often do we get to tell our friends what to do? This is what we need to remember about our friendship with Jesus.

Even though He calls us "friend," the following point is also true.

Jesus's friends are still His servants, and He is still the master. I once heard someone say it this way: A master (or boss) can be a friend with a servant (or employee), but it is always understood to be an unequal relationship. If the master is not the servant's friend, he will just boss the person around. But if the master is a friend, he does so differently. How so?

Jesus tells His friends what God wants them to know. Jesus had that kind of relationship with His disciples. He didn't keep stuff to Himself, but what God the Father told Him, He passed on. He wanted them to understand the will of God and experience the rich life for which they had been saved. They weren't just pawns in a cosmic game of chess He was playing; a relationship with them was the very reason He played the game (John 3:16).

This isn't something that stopped with the disciples either. We have the very same access to what God wants us to know and how He wants us to live (2 Pet. 1:3). As we treasure the Word of God, we get to know our master and friend Jesus more and more.

Jesus gets to pick His friends. Most friendships are two people saying to each other, "I pick you." Our friendship with Jesus is different. As the master, He does the picking, just as God did with Abraham (Isa. 41:8) and Moses (Exod. 33:11). This should cause us to be amazed. With all the sinful nonsense I have going on in my life, He picks me! Even when people could look at me and say of Jesus, "Look at Him! A glutton and a drunkard, a friend of Noel's!" (see Luke 7:34), He picks me. And He picks you too.

That's a good friend to have.

DISCUSSION QUESTIONS

What do you think when you hear the word *religion*? Do you think of Christianity as a religion? Do you believe *religion* to be negative, positive, or neutral? Why?

"Christianity isn't a religion! It's a relationship!" Have you ever heard this? Said this? Talk about what this means to you or what it might mean to others around you.

What is the difference between "true religion" and "self-made religion"? Which of the two has your own experience of Christianity been?

Have you had personal experience with other world religions and the "ladders" they have? Discuss your own experience or that of those you know who are working on the dos and don'ts of other religions.

Do you agree that in Christianity there is nothing for us to do because it has all been done for us? Have a look at Ephesians 2:1–9 again, then talk about what this message means to you.

The author's experience at Pizza Hut, when his father extended unexpected mercy and forgiveness, made a huge impact on him. His father's actions pointed him to the gospel in a way that mere words never could have. Has someone ever demonstrated the gospel to you in a powerful way? What was it like, and how did it influence you?

Every single aspect of our salvation—being saved, grace, faith, and even keeping yourself saved—is a free gift. You are not responsible for these things; God is. What does this mean to you?

Have you added any rules to your life that you think would make God happier? Talk about some of the rules or practices that you or Christians you know have added to their faith. Are these rules good or bad?

God uses our human relationships as metaphors to show us how a relationship with Him should be. For example, He is our Father; we are His children. Our fellow Christians are brothers and sisters.

How has your own family dynamic affected how you think of God as your heavenly Father or the church as your extended family?

"Adoption is a beautiful gospel picture." The author uses the example of a family's adoption process to show how we are trapped here while God is somewhere else, yet how we have the Spirit with us to point us to our true, eternal home. Like the children's guardians in Mexico did, how does the Spirit "show us pictures" or "tell us stories" about what is to come?

John 15:12–21 talks about Jesus as our friend. Reread this passage, then discuss how our relationship with Jesus should look in terms of being His friend.

The friendship Jesus has with us is different in some major ways from the relationships we typically have with our other friends. We are friends with Jesus, but we are not equals. He is still the master. He tells us what God wants to communicate to us. And He gets to pick us. Do you think of Jesus as a friend?

CHAPTER 5

SET FREE *FROM SIN*

"Yeahbut."

It's a deadly little word that isn't even a word.

Yeahbut essentially declares, "I believe what you are saying is true, but I don't know how to synthesize this truth with something else I also believe to be true." If you listen carefully, you will hear *yeahbuts* all the time. They pop up in casual conversation and arguments at work, and you will definitely hear one when you talk with a Christian about freedom.

"*Yeah*, I believe Jesus set me free (and I may even be willing to concede I am free from the Law and religion), *but* does that mean I am free to sin?"

In other words, "I'm not *really* free, am I?" The unspoken logic behind the question goes something like this: if I am truly set free, the best use of my freedom is to sin. By asking the question, we betray that the thing we want most is to sin without consequence.

If we can't use our freedom as a hall pass or a "get out of jail free" card, what good is it?

Deep down, we all want to sin without consequence, which is the problem with the question "Yeah, I believe Jesus set me free, but does that mean I am free to sin?"

Of course, not everyone who asks this question is asking it because they want to run around and sin with impunity. Often, the people asking it are pointing their fingers at someone else and don't want that person *over there* to sin. They would never dream of abusing their freedom that way. But *that guy over there*? Of course *he* would!

Now, beyond the sheer offensiveness of this entire thing, there's a bigger problem. The question, no matter who is asking it, is evident that we are viewing our sin from, you guessed it, inside the box. We talked about this already in chapter 2, remember? Because we can't conceive of a world outside the box, the freedom we think we want is naturally the freedom to sin.

But let's not avoid the question, because it's still important.

IS IT OKAY TO SIN?

The very first person ever hit with the question "Is it okay to sin?" (that we have record of) was the apostle Paul, and he addressed it head on in Romans 5–6. In Romans 5, he reminded his readers that Jesus's obedience was so perfect that it was enough for everybody (Rom. 5:18). That obedience, culminating in His death, burial, and resurrection, forever secures our new position outside of the box. Once Paul had laid that groundwork, he knew the *yeahbut* was coming because his readers were conditionally still in the box.

> What shall we say then? Are we to continue in sin
> that grace may abound? (Rom. 6:1)

In fact, that's kind of the snarky way of saying, "More sin means more grace, am I right?" Wink, wink, nudge, nudge … Paul's answer was quick, clear, and emphatic:

> By no means! (Rom. 6:2)

In fact, he said it twice (Rom. 6:15).

With this statement, Paul was declaring that even asking the question betrayed a fundamental misunderstanding of what Jesus had accomplished and that it therefore just didn't make sense.

The very reason Jesus went to the cross is because sin is so vile, so evil, that it needed cosmic intervention (Rom. 6:23). Now that sin is defeated, it would be ridiculous to say, "*Yeahbut*, can I still do that vile and evil thing I love to do that killed Jesus? That would be great fun!" Now most of us aren't that blunt (or that self-aware), but deep down we wonder, *Is God still pleased with me when I sin?*

You see, we know ourselves pretty well, and we know that we are always sinning. We also know that sin is pretty displeasing to God, to put it mildly (Ps. 5:4). That causes us to get stuck in this little theological cul-de-sac where we wonder if God is truly pleased with us when we are sinning. And because He is all-powerful and could snap His fingers to get us to stop sinning, obviously this must be our fault. If that is the case, we are responsible for keeping ourselves saved, right? And around and around the cul-de-sac we go.

This is why good theology matters so much.

At the core, this entire line of thinking wrestles with a fundamental question: Who's doing the work here—God or me?

During Paul's conversion, Jesus provided a picture that may be helpful in answering this question. Jesus said to Paul (then called Saul), "Why are you persecuting me? It is hard for you to kick against the goads" (Acts 26:14).

What does that mean? What is a goad, and why would you kick it? A goad was a pointy stick used to direct an animal, such as a sheep or a horse, by poking it. An animal that would kick at the goads would only be prolonging the inevitable and causing itself pain.

What was Jesus getting at? Well, Paul was persecuting the church at the same time he was studying what they were saying. He was a very highly educated man, and it's certain he was processing the theology of this new faith, even if just to disprove it.

As he wrestled with their beliefs, the proof for Jesus was mounting in his brain, and the Holy Spirit was doing a transforming work in his spirit. He was fighting against his conscience. He was fighting against his own intellect. He was fighting against the overwhelming proof that Jesus was really the Messiah the Jews had been waiting for, that His sinless life was necessary to fulfill the Law, that His death on the cross could truly bear the sins of the world, and that His resurrection would conquer sin, Satan, and death. Ultimately, Paul was fighting against the faith God was giving him to believe.

Paul was kicking against the goads.

We do the same thing—and not just when we are being saved. We do it for the rest of our lives here on earth. Paul himself said:

> For I do not understand my own actions. For I do not do what I want, but I do the very thing I hate. Now if I do what I do not want, I agree with the law, that it is good. So now it is no longer I who do it, but sin that dwells within me. For I know that nothing good dwells in me, that is, in my flesh. For I have the desire to do what is right, but not the ability to carry it out. For I do not do the good I want, but the evil I do not want is what I keep on doing. Now if I do what I do not want, it is no longer I who do it, but sin that dwells within me.
>
> So I find it to be a law that when I want to do right, evil lies close at hand. For I delight in the law of God, in my inner being, but I see in my members another law waging war against the law of my mind and making me captive to the law of sin that dwells in my members. Wretched man that I am! Who will deliver me from this body of death? (Rom. 7:15–24)

Wow. Paul was beating himself up pretty badly, wasn't he? It was as though he was kicking against the goads of his sanctification. He summed it all up with this "man at the end of his rope" cry: "Who will deliver me from this body of death?" And the answer?

> Thanks be to God through Jesus Christ our Lord! So then, I myself serve the law of God with my mind, but with my flesh I serve the law of sin.
>
> There is therefore now no condemnation for those who are in Christ Jesus. (Rom. 7:25—8:1)

Who would save him? Jesus. Jesus, who had already saved him (justification), would save him (sanctification). And so he could declare, in the midst of his agonizing wrestling match with sin: "I am not condemned!"

Let this sink in. Fight with it if you have to, but don't let go. You are not condemned. Even when you sin. And if I may be so bold to say, you are not condemned *especially* when you sin.

Now before you crucify me, let me get my heresy out on the table. What did Paul say way back in Romans 5? "God shows his love for us in that *while we were still sinners*, Christ died for us" (v. 8). It is in our sin that we are *least* condemned because that's precisely why and when Jesus came to save us. He didn't come to save us from our momentary diversions into righteous living but from our consistently wretched and pathetic attempts at living apart from Him! Our sin is what condemns us, and as Terry Virgo[1] said, "You can't overcome condemnation with sanctification. That's what justification is for."

The best way to grapple with this is to go back to the definition of sin we introduced earlier in the book: "Sin is any failure to reflect the image of God in nature, attitude, or action."

An understanding of our position in Christ necessarily affects our entire relationship with sin because Jesus changes our nature, our attitude, and our actions.

JESUS CHANGES OUR SINFUL NATURE

Pop quiz time! Which of these is more important: who we are or what we do? Down through history, the predominant viewpoint has been that *what we do* determines *who we are.* We've all heard the old adage, "You are what you eat." This isn't a new school of thought. Aristotle wrote, "We are what we repeatedly do."[2] A recent TED talk declared, "You are what you tweet."[3] Each one of these proclamations, while carrying a significant nugget of truth, gets the core message of the gospel backward. Frank Zappa, of all people, got it right: "You are what you is."[4] In other words, it's not what we do that determines who we are; rather, who we are determines what we do. This is the biblical paradigm.

JESUS CHANGES OUR SINFUL ATTITUDES

Because we are new creations that think differently, our attitude toward sin changes. I was once asked by a couple to perform their wedding, and I had to tell them I couldn't do so with a clear conscience because the woman professed to be a follower of Jesus and her fiancé didn't. I went for a long walk with the guy and explained where I was coming from and why I couldn't perform the wedding. I then shared the gospel with him, and he respectfully listened and very graciously thanked me for my time. I assumed that would be the end of it, but it wasn't.

A few months later, he called me and told me he had a problem. Here's what he said, nearly word for word: "I decided to place my faith in Jesus and become a Christian, but I haven't told my fiancée because I don't want her to think I did it just so she would feel better about marrying me." I assured him this was a wonderful thing and he should talk to her right away, but apparently the problem was deeper. After becoming a Christian, he became convicted that they needed to remain sexually pure before their wedding, and that proved difficult because they were living together. He wanted to ask her to move in with her parents halfway across the country until their wedding day to help them remain sexually pure, and he wasn't sure how she was going to react.

His new nature caused him to have a new attitude toward sin. In all of our conversations, I had never talked with him about his sex life or his living situation. Rather, I had talked with him about his need for Jesus. When he became a Christian, Jesus changed him deep inside so that he wanted to live a different life.

JESUS CHANGES OUR SINFUL ACTIONS

There is a common *yeahbut* verse that gets thrown around a lot when you start talking about freedom:

> What good is it, my brothers, if someone says he
> has faith but does not have works? Can that faith
> save him? (James 2:14)

I've had that one thrown at me more than any other when talking with people about their freedom in Christ. And it is a tough one—if you don't read it in context. Once you do, it becomes crystal clear. Let's zoom out a bit:

> For whoever keeps the whole law but fails in one
> point has become guilty of all of it. For he who
> said, "Do not commit adultery," also said, "Do
> not murder." If you do not commit adultery but
> do murder, you have become a transgressor of the
> law. So speak and so act as those who are to be
> judged under the law of liberty. For judgment is
> without mercy to one who has shown no mercy.
> Mercy triumphs over judgment.
>
> What good is it, my brothers, if someone
> says he has faith but does not have works? Can
> that faith save him? (James 2:10–14)

This passage actually starts out sounding even worse. James makes the case that if you have ever committed adultery (and let's not forget that Jesus says in Matthew 5:28 you are guilty of that one if you even look at someone with lust in your heart), you are just as bad as a murderer. Why? Because the law is a single unit!

You break one part of it, and it's as if you have broken it all. There is no grading on a curve. It's like getting a 36 or a 0 on your ACT. It's like getting a 180 or a 0 on your LSAT. It's like driving a single mile per hour over the speed limit one time and being guilty of every moving violation in the book.

One sin makes you a sinner.

But that's not the whole story, is it?

You know it's not; it's just the beginning.

James wants that point to really sink in so he can throw down this doozy: "So speak and so act *as those who are to be judged under the law of liberty.*" Let's say it a different way: "Good thing you aren't under the law! So act like it. Speak and act like a free person. You have been given mercy instead of judgment, so offer the same to others."

When our nature changes, our attitudes and actions are not far behind. Understanding our new position helps us comprehend a lot of these tricky verses. Let's look at a few more of them.

> But I say, walk by the Spirit, and you will not gratify the desires of the flesh. For the desires of the flesh are against the Spirit, and the desires of the Spirit are against the flesh, for these are opposed to each other, to keep you from doing the things you want to do. But if you are led by the Spirit, you are not under the law. Now the works of the flesh are evident: sexual immorality, impurity, sensuality, idolatry, sorcery, enmity, strife, jealousy, fits of anger, rivalries, dissensions,

divisions, envy, drunkenness, orgies, and things like these. I warn you, as I warned you before, that those who do such things will not inherit the kingdom of God. But the fruit of the Spirit is love, joy, peace, patience, kindness, goodness, faithfulness, gentleness, self-control; against such things there is no law. And those who belong to Christ Jesus have crucified the flesh with its passions and desires. (Gal. 5:16–24)

At first glance, this passage looks like a big ol' don't-do list followed by a big ol' to-do list. It's natural to read it and do a quick calculation of how you are doing. The one that really gets me is "things like these" on the don't list. I am convinced I am doing and thinking about sinful things that land me on the don't list.

But what is this passage really saying? Well, let's look at the bookends:

Bookend 1: "But I say, walk by the Spirit, and you will not gratify the desires of the flesh."
Bookend 2: "And those who belong to Christ Jesus have crucified the flesh with its passions and desires."

Everything else sits in between!

When you begin to catch this pattern, you will see it again and again in Paul's writings. He never talks about sin in the lives of believers without reminding them about what is true of them as followers of Jesus. Here he isn't *prescribing* a way of living as much as he is *describing* what happens in the life of a follower of Jesus. If we think perfect performance in these areas is necessary in this life, then we are in big trouble because none of us can live up to this standard. This isn't a standard of life we have to run after; it's what Jesus does in the life of His people.

But what about verses like these:

> Do you not know that in a race all the runners run, but only one receives the prize? So run that you may obtain it. Every athlete exercises self-control in all things. They do it to receive a perishable wreath, but we an imperishable. So I do not run aimlessly; I do not box as one beating the air. But I discipline my body and keep it under control, lest after preaching to others I myself should be disqualified. (1 Cor. 9:24–27)

Seems pretty straightforward, right? I can be disqualified if I don't *do* enough of the right things. But is that what Paul is saying? Again, it helps to zoom out. Here are the verses right before the ones we just read (and they should look familiar):

> For though I am free from all, I have made myself a servant to all, that I might win more of them. To the Jews I became as a Jew, in order to win Jews.

> To those under the law I became as one under
> the law (though not being myself under the law)
> that I might win those under the law. To those
> outside the law I became as one outside the law
> (not being outside the law of God but under the
> law of Christ) that I might win those outside the
> law. To the weak I became weak, that I might win
> the weak. I have become all things to all people,
> that by all means I might save some. I do it all for
> the sake of the gospel, that I may share with them
> in its blessings. (1 Cor. 9:19–23)

This passage is actually pretty remarkable now that we see the context. The discipline, the running, the boxing that Paul is doing *is living out his freedom in Christ!* How?

He acted like a Jew when he was around Jews.

He placed himself under the Law when he was around those who felt they were still under it.

He lived outside of the Law when he was around those who didn't.

He became weak when he was around the weak.

Essentially, Paul didn't live by some long list of dos and don'ts. What drove him forward was not an effort to make himself more righteous or somehow hold on to his righteousness. Rather, the righteousness he had already been given drove him to love people and to live in such a way that others would become curious about Jesus and the freedom He offers. Paul's race was to invite other people to race with him.

Let's look at a trickier passage and one that starts with a very important phrase:

> Let not sin therefore reign in your mortal body, to make you obey its passions. Do not present your members to sin as instruments for unrighteousness, but present yourselves to God as those who have been brought from death to life, and your members to God as instruments for righteousness. (Rom. 6:12–13)

"Let not sin …" That's a remarkable statement. It means what it says: You can make a decision now. You have been set free from the power of sin, so you can actually say yes to Jesus and no to sin. You can, because of Jesus, choose not to sin. You can choose not to present your members to sin. How is that possible? "For sin will have no dominion over you, since you are not under law but under grace" (Rom. 6:14).

But let's get really honest. We like sin. We want to sin. That's because we still have the flesh. Which means we are going to stumble. And when we do, nothing, *nothing*, I have just said changes one bit. Jesus Christ has set you free from the eternal consequences of sin, Jesus Christ has set you free from the guilt that comes with sin, and Jesus Christ has set you free from the power of sin. As the author of Hebrews put it so eloquently, "By a single offering he has perfected for all time those who are being sanctified" (10:14).

You have *been* perfected (justified).

You are *being* sanctified.

You are both *outside* of the box and *inside* the box.

Sin has no dominion over you, *and* you are still going to sin.

The apostle John said it this way: "I am writing these things to you so that you may not sin. But if anyone does sin, we have an advocate with the Father, Jesus Christ the righteous" (1 John 2:1).

You shouldn't sin.

Yeah, you are gonna sin.

Jesus has you covered.

Sometimes the math of our salvation just doesn't compute in our finite brains. Thankfully, the longer we follow Jesus, the more this whole thing begins to make sense, because God continues to do a work inside us every day. I love how Bryan Chapell put it: "There is a chemistry of the heart (we are united to Christ) that is greater than the math of the mind (I am saved so I can sin)."[5]

In the cage match of the Christian life, chemistry beats math, but it takes the whole five rounds. These two duke it out our whole lives, which is what makes us such complicated beings. It's why I like to refer to myself as a "recovering hypocrite." I don't claim to have this all together, but that's okay. If you are around me long enough, I'm going to fail you. I'll say stupid stuff, I'll take three steps back in my maturity, and so will you. But that's part of the beauty of the gospel! It's not about us or what we have done. It's about Jesus.

So let's boil this whole thing down into a crazy, seemingly contradictory equation.

Because of Jesus, God is pleased with me.

Nevertheless, God is not pleased with my sin.

However, Jesus has already handled my sin.

Therefore, all that is left is that God is pleased with me.

Sometimes we feel as though God is up in heaven, saying to Himself, "If I had known [insert your name here] was going to sin like *that* after she became a Christian, I certainly wouldn't have saved her." But that is a lie straight from the pits of hell.

Jesus has saved you, He is saving you, and He will save you.

Here's a promise to cling to every day:

> I am sure of this, that he who began a good work in you will bring it to completion at the day of Jesus Christ. (Phil. 1:6)

Who began the work in your life? Jesus.

Who will bring it to completion? Jesus.

When will He do it? On His day.

So yeah, we obey Jesus, but in the words of C. S. Lewis, we obey "in a new way, a less worried way."[6]

DISCUSSION QUESTIONS

When faced with the question "Who's doing the work here—God or me?" how would you answer? Does the way you live your life agree with your answer?

Paul (Saul) was "kicking against the goads" when he was fighting against God and the faith God was giving him. Why would he do this? Have you ever done this? If so, how and why?

Do you believe, truly believe, that you are not condemned when you sin? Is this ever hard to accept, both for yourself and for other believers? Why or why not?

What is more important to you: who you are or what you do?

When people become Christian, Jesus changes them inside and they *want* to live a different life. How have you seen this play out in the lives of Christians around you? Where have you seen this happen in your own life?

"Paul didn't live by some long list of dos and don'ts. What drove him forward was not an effort to make himself more righteous or somehow hold on to his righteousness. Rather, the righteousness he had already been given drove him to love people and live in such a way that others would become curious about Jesus and the freedom he offers." What are some ways that Christians can become "all things to all people, that by all means [we] might save some" (1 Cor. 9:22)? What are some freedoms you could sacrifice in order to love others better and point them to Jesus?

"Christianity isn't about us or what we have done. It's about Jesus." Do most Christians you know admit that they are messed up and always will be? Do you think this is helpful or hurtful for Christians? How about you—do you ever feel pressure to make it seem like you have everything together?

Do you believe that even when you sin, God is still pleased with you? Talk about how we can know this is true.

What is the difference between conviction and condemnation? When you sin, do you feel condemned? How can you actively fight that?

PART THREE

SET FREE *FOR FREEDOM*

For freedom Christ has set us free.

Galatians 5:1

After nearly forty years of living in the same place, my father-in-law downsized from a large suburban house to a two-bedroom condo. As he was cleaning out the garage, he texted me a picture of several vintage Snap-on toolboxes and asked if I wanted them, along with all the tools they contained.

I was ecstatic because my father-in-law had owned a car-repair shop for a number of years and I couldn't wait to get my hands on all his tools. That was until I showed up at his house and cracked open the toolboxes. Mixed in with the Crescent wrenches and air-compressor fittings were, well, I don't know what they were. There were more tools I didn't recognize than tools I did.

One by one, I would pull something weird looking out of a drawer and ask Dad, "What do I do with this?"

"I don't know. Just throw it away."

It felt strange throwing so many tools away. To this day, I wonder if I pitched something I will end up needing.

That's how we often treat our freedom in Christ. We don't know what to do with it, so we toss it aside without realizing how valuable it is and how helpful it will be.

In this section, we will take a look at how Jesus has set us free so that we can actually experience freedom.

CHAPTER 6

SET FREE *FOR FREEDOM FROM GUILT*

A lot of little kids are afraid of monsters that reportedly live under their beds. I never really had that issue. In fact, I would have slept like a baby every night if it weren't for the object of my fear.

I was afraid of God.

After a long day of being a kid, I would lie down in my bunk bed, and before drifting off to sleep, I would mentally replay my day. This daily ritual didn't focus on the good stuff very often. It was more like a "sin recap." Visions of sassing my mom (that's what she called it), throwing darts at one of my brothers (I really did), and generally tormenting my other brother would make up the highlight reel. As I lay on my Batman sheets, staring at the ceiling, I would fitfully wonder what would happen to me if I died in my sleep. I had never known anyone who died in their sleep, but somehow it was my greatest fear. I was afraid because

I was convinced I would not see a pleased look on God's face at the pearly gates—if I made it even that far.

To make sure I would be good with Him if I met my untimely demise, I would confess all of my sins from that day and ask forgiveness one at a time. After I had exhausted all of my conscious wrongdoings, I would begin to worry about the sins I had forgotten about or not even realized I had committed. That's when my heart would *really* begin to race. It became customary for me to close my frightful prayer time with the line "And if I have forgotten anything, please forgive me for that too. Amen."

By the time I got into high school, I paid very little attention to my sin and so I slept much better. But trouble struck when I reached college. You see, it was then that I began to systematically read through the Bible and really understand what God expected of me. The more I read, the more I came to the painful realization of how far I fell short from His standard. As a newly passionate follower of Jesus, I was acutely aware of the severe punishment He took on my behalf. The crown of thorns, the whips, the cross, and the general humiliation He faced were the result of my behavior.

This knowledge had a very real and unexpected consequence: guilt.

Every single misstep I made in my faith caused me to beat myself up, not just at night, but all day long. I would ride my bike to class wondering why I couldn't get my act together. Jesus had done so much for me; why wasn't I able to be a better Christian in return? What was wrong with me?

Over the past twenty-five years, I have talked with many Christians who have experienced the same thing. The very week I began to write this chapter, a guy found me in the church lobby and asked if we could talk. He had recently become a Christian and was finding it hard to kick a sinful pattern he had developed over many years. The constant remorse was killing him. He asked me, point blank, "Is it normal for a Christian to feel so guilty all the time?"

Unfortunately, the answer is yes.

But it shouldn't be. For all the reasons we have already covered in this book, it shouldn't be. But it is. Why?

There are a lot of reasons for our guilt, but one really sticks out—we have an enemy, a very real enemy, and he wants to steal our freedom. The Bible calls him "the accuser of our brothers" who "accuses them day and night before our God" (Rev. 12:10). That's an eye-opening statement, isn't it? It would seem that Satan's main job description (and evidently his favorite hobby, too, since he does it all day and all night) is to accuse. And who does he accuse? Christians! And where does he do it? Before our God.

We get a pretty good picture of Satan putting this into action in the Old Testament, where we are introduced to a man named Job. God described this man as "blameless and upright, one who feared God and turned away from evil" (Job 1:1). How would you like that character reference on your résumé? Not only was this dude's behavior above reproach, but he was superwealthy. That means he was probably even more godly than we think (not because he was wealthy, but because wealthy people have a really hard time being godly; check out Matt. 19:24).

This rather remarkable man caught not only God's eye but Satan's as well. Check out this exchange:

> The LORD said to Satan, "From where have you come?" Satan answered the LORD and said, "From going to and fro on the earth, and from walking up and down on it." And the LORD said to Satan, "Have you considered my servant Job, that there is none like him on the earth, a blameless and upright man, who fears God and turns away from evil?" Then Satan answered the LORD and said, "Does Job fear God for no reason? Have you not put a hedge around him and his house and all that he has, on every side? You have blessed the work of his hands, and his possessions have increased in the land. But stretch out your hand and touch all that he has, and he will curse you to your face." (Job 1:7–11)

Satan had seen Job's stellar character but didn't believe he was actually a righteous man. He chalked up his good behavior to nothing more than being a spoiled brat. He thought God was treating Job like a mom bribing her toddler with a piece of candy. Job's business was booming, his family loved him, his employees loved him and thought he was the man, he threw lavish parties to celebrate his great life; of course he blessed God! With all that going for a person, who wouldn't?

After leveling his accusation of unfairness against God, Satan laid down a challenge: smite the man. Satan was convinced that if God caused Job pain, Job would curse God in return. The rest of the book of Job details his life falling to pieces while he grappled with the reasons why. At one point, he even went so far as to say God was treating him unfairly because he *didn't feel guilty*. In Job's mind, the circumstances of his life had a direct correlation with his performance before God, and he couldn't reconcile the two.

In the book of Zechariah we have a similar picture of Satan doing his accusation work with another Old Testament character.

> Then he showed me Joshua the high priest standing before the angel of the LORD, and Satan standing at his right hand to accuse him. (3:1)

This time the accused wasn't some random rich dude. Rather, it was the high priest of God, the man with the terrifying job of standing before God as humankind's representative. Joshua was kind of a big deal. While he was busy working away at his job, Satan was busy at his, standing next to God and accusing one of God's people. And this time around, the plot thickened.

> And the LORD said to Satan, "The LORD rebuke you, O Satan! The LORD who has chosen Jerusalem rebuke you! Is not this a brand plucked from the fire?" Now Joshua was standing before the angel, clothed with filthy garments. And the

> angel said to those who were standing before him,
> "Remove the filthy garments from him." And to
> him he said, "Behold, I have taken your iniquity
> away from you, and I will clothe you with pure
> vestments." And I said, "Let them put a clean tur-
> ban on his head." So they put a clean turban on
> his head and clothed him with garments. And the
> angel of the LORD was standing by. (Zech. 3:2–5)

Joshua, despite being the high priest, didn't get the rosy character reference Job got. Instead of righteous, he was described as
dirty—filthy, in fact. But God took care of this. He cleaned up
Joshua and symbolically cleaned up the entire nation of Israel in
the process.

This is the pattern we see again and again in Scripture. Satan
accuses God's people of being low-down, dirty sinners (whether
righteous or not) while God is busy cleaning them up from their
sin. Now don't miss a very important point: in both of these
instances, Satan is accusing God's people. We don't have any record
of him accusing non-Christians or trying to mess with the enemies
of God. Why? Because if he did and they were convicted of their
sin, they would run in search of a savior, and that could very well
lead them right to Jesus!

God's people are Satan's target. Satan reserves his accusations
for those God loves and Jesus has saved. He blasts people who are
indwelled with the Holy Spirit and are therefore conscious of their
sin. You see what that means? If you are constantly feeling guilty,

as bizarre as it seems, you should at least be encouraged and feel safe and secure in your salvation! If you weren't a Christian, Satan wouldn't bother with you at all.

BEING GUILTY AND FEELING GUILTY AREN'T THE SAME THING

As followers of Jesus, we can safely assume that Satan's strategy of accusation remains the same today. He wants us to feel guilty even though Jesus has cleaned us up and set us free. And let's be honest: accusing us of sin and making us feel guilty is like shooting fish in a barrel. Every time we mess up, Satan accuses us of being worthless scum, and we believe him.

The more we struggle with the same old sins, the more we tend to believe his lies. And yes, make no mistake, his accusations against us are lies. Jesus says Satan "does not stand in the truth, because *there is no truth in him*. When he lies, he speaks out of his own character, for he is a liar and the father of lies" (John 8:44).

But wait. If Satan is just pointing out sin that we have really committed, how can we say he is lying? Well, it's important to know what we mean by "guilt." Guilt comes in two broad categories, which can be described as "legal guilt" (being guilty) and "emotional guilt" (feeling guilty). Most of us take the same path from guilty to not guilty, and it looks like this:

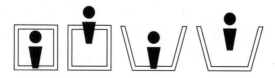

STEP ONE: TRAPPED (BEING GUILTY AND FEELING NOT GUILTY)

Born with a sin nature we inherited from our great-granddaddy Adam, we all start in chains (or "trapped in the box"). As Scripture makes abundantly clear, we are all guilty in our sin and of our sins, and our consciences attest to that guilt. Unfortunately, sin has also wreaked havoc on how we process our guilt. The apostle Paul said it this way:

> To the pure, all things are pure, but to the defiled and unbelieving, nothing is pure; but both their minds and their consciences are defiled. They profess to know God, but they deny him by their works. They are detestable, disobedient, unfit for any good work. (Titus 1:15–16)

What an interesting and frightening assessment. Scores of people think they know God, but they don't. They often feel they are right with God because they are pretty good people who recycle, don't abuse their pets, and only drink fair-trade coffee. On a cosmic scale, they feel as though they have done more right than wrong, and yet Paul says nothing they do is truly pure and "they deny [God] by their works. They are detestable, dis-obedient, unfit for any good work." How can this be, when they feel as though they are doing the right thing? It's because their consciences are defiled by sin. In 1 Timothy, we see a great word picture that diagnoses some consciences as "seared" (4:2).

Have you ever taken an impatient bite from a slice of pizza that just came out of the oven? If you have, you know what comes next. The instant the boiling-hot cheese touches the roof of your mouth, it burns the skin to a crisp, and little pieces of skin hang down into your mouth like the melted cheese that started the whole process. Fortunately, the mozzarella also sears your nerve endings so the pain is over quickly. Unfortunately, it sears your taste buds too, and the penalty for your impatience is that you can, for a while, no longer taste *anything*.

That's what happens with our consciences when we sin again and again in the same way. Right and wrong begin to taste the same, and even the right we do has a little taste of wrong in it. But because we can't tell the difference, we assume everything is okay.

In Romans, Paul goes so far as to say there comes a point where God gives people "up in the lusts of their hearts to impurity, to the dishonoring of their bodies among themselves, because they exchanged the truth about God for a lie and worshiped and served the creature rather than the Creator" (1:24–25).

On those rare occasions when we realize we have developed a pattern of sin, we are often quick to deflect responsibility onto someone else because, obviously, we can't possibly be at fault for what we do. It would seem that even when we are (legally) guilty, we typically don't feel (emotionally) guilty. It's like the countless parade of celebrities who declare after a scandal, "Only God can judge me," without realizing He actually does. We would all do well to remember Jesus's warning: "Do not fear those who kill the body but cannot kill the soul. Rather fear him who can destroy both soul and body in hell" (Matt. 10:28). And in case you missed it, Jesus is talking about God here. It's appropriate to be afraid of God when we are guilty of our sins.

STEP TWO: CONVICTED (BEING GUILTY AND FEELING GUILTY)

This is a crucial, and usually short-lived, step in which we become convicted of our sin through the Scripture (2 Tim. 3:16) and the Holy Spirit (John 16:8). I have long loved the imagery Francis Thompson used to describe God's pursuit of sinful people through this step. He referred to God as "The Hound of Heaven."[1] In his 182-line poem of the same name (which you would do well to read, although it can be a bit tough to work through), this tormented, drug-addicted poet wrote:

From those strong Feet that followed,
>   followed after.
>   But with unhurrying chase,
>   And unperturbéd pace,
> Deliberate speed, majestic instancy,
>   They beat—and a Voice beat
>   More instant than the Feet—
> "All things betray thee, who betrayest Me."

This "Hound of Heaven" is the Holy Spirit who convicts us of our sin. Over time, He patiently builds His case in our spirit until we become acutely aware of our sin. No longer living in blissful ignorance, we see our sin for what it is, and the need for a savior wells up inside of us. We are no longer just legally guilty, but now we know it emotionally. Of course, we likely don't realize the depths of our sin at this point (or ever), but we know we have violated God's will for our lives. It's interesting that Leviticus 5 lays out penalties for both the knowing and the unknowing breaking of God's law. Just as the old Latin legal phrase declares, "*Ignorantia juris non excusat*"—ignorance of the law excuses not.

If we stay ignorant of our sin, there is no benefit here or in the next life. As Paul wrote:

> For godly grief produces a repentance that leads to salvation without regret, whereas worldly grief produces death. (2 Cor. 7:10)

STEP THREE: MISERABLE (NOT BEING GUILTY AND FEELING GUILTY ANYWAY)

> If we confess our sins, he is faithful and just to
> forgive us our sins and to cleanse us from all
> unrighteousness. (1 John 1:9)

In that moment of salvation, our legal guilt is taken care of, once for all time. Jesus unchains us and sets us free. Usually, this comes with some legitimate excitement, a newfound joy and purpose, and a period of telling a lot of people about Jesus. But for many people, this is when their internal battle begins in earnest, because this is when our enemy begins to get his accusation on.

I suspect this step is the reason a great many people picked up this book. It's certainly one of the biggest reasons I wrote it. I have talked to too many people too many times who live their entire Christian lives stuck right here within inches of feeling free, and it's tragic. Why? "For freedom Christ has set us free."

The reason so many people get stuck in this place is actually a noble one: we want to live for Jesus. Everything inside of us (including our new self and the Holy Spirit) is calling out for our condition to sync up with our position. So when we sin, we feel really, really guilty, and we beat ourselves up for it. You see, the fundamental reason you feel guilty is because your conscience is no longer defiled! You know right from wrong, you know what sin is, and you know when you do it. This makes you an easy target for the accuser.

We even start to beat ourselves up for things that are not actually sinful. Paul talked about this in 1 Corinthians 8, concerning an issue that was a really big deal to the Corinthian believers: food sacrificed to idols. Now to us, this doesn't feel like a big deal, but it was huge for them.

You see, the people who ran the pagan temples in Corinth were like the mafia, and they had a great racket going. First off, they made tons of money from temple prostitution. Second, they found a way to make people pay for something they already owned. Here's how it worked: If you wanted to "appease the gods" (maybe you needed a good harvest or a firstborn son or something like that), you would bring a sacrifice to the temple. Not any sacrifice, though; you had to bring an animal. Not just any animal, either; you had to bring the best animal from your flock.

Imagine you are an extremely poor family and you are counting on a good harvest to both feed your family and sell at the market. To get this crop, you need the gods on your side, so you take your best, fattest goat to the temple. The so-called priests kill your goat and chop it up into three pieces. The first piece they ceremonially burn on the altar to a fake god. The second piece they cook up and serve back to you as part of a feast you participate in as an act of worship. Of course, you have to pay for this meal. The third piece they pass to a guy in the back. That guy takes the meat out the back door to the market where they sell it to people buying their groceries.

So, in the temple, you could pay for lunch made from meats you provided. Then, on your way out, you could stop at the marketplace and buy another chunk of meat you just brought in the front door. It was a brilliant scam.

Because of how obviously sketchy this whole thing was, the Christians in Corinth were concerned about being guilty by association by participating in any way. They knew they weren't supposed to take part in phase 1 (idol worship), but what about phase 2 (eating at the temple) or phase 3 (eating potentially tainted food they purchased in the marketplace)? They were feeling guilty, but they weren't sure if they should.

Paul broke it down for them:

> Now concerning food offered to idols: we know
> that "all of us possess knowledge." This "knowl-
> edge" puffs up, but love builds up. (1 Cor. 8:1)

He started out by saying, "There is some stuff that all of us know." For instance, what is two plus two? It's four. We all know this. This type of knowledge is commonplace. But then there is the type of knowledge that a few people possess and others don't have, such as the knowledge auto mechanics have. I am a car-guy wannabe. But there are times my mechanic brings up stuff that completely loses me. For all I know, he could be telling me to replace the flux capacitor on my Toyota. In those moments of insecurity, I am so tempted to prove that I am also well versed in a very specific field of knowledge by declaring, "I bet you don't even know what anthropomorphism is!" *Boom!*

Here's the problem. Paul was diagnosing for the Corinthians. When you know something and you know that other people don't know what you know, it has a sinful effect on you. It puffs you up. You get a big head. You get arrogant. But Paul said there was an antidote to this arrogance: love. Paul's ultimate example of this was God:

> If anyone imagines that he knows something,
> he does not yet know as he ought to know.
> But if anyone loves God, he is known by God.
> (1 Cor. 8:2–3)

One Bible commentator nailed this when he said, "Ignorance does not know that it does not know. True knowledge does not know and knows it."[2] Every one of us has gaps in our knowledge; there's stuff we just don't know. But that's okay, because we are known by God. He knows what we don't know and He loves us in our ignorance. His love supersedes our lack of knowledge.

Paul then took his readers back to their guilt.

> Therefore, as to the eating of food offered to idols,
> we know that "an idol has no real existence," and

> that "there is no God but one." For although
> there may be so-called gods in heaven or on
> earth—as indeed there are many "gods" and
> many "lords"—yet for us there is one God, the
> Father, from whom are all things and for whom
> we exist, and one Lord, Jesus Christ, through
> whom are all things and through whom we exist.
> (1 Cor. 8:4–6)

Simply put, Paul says that we can know two things related to idolatry: "an idol has no real existence" and "there is no God but one." Idols aren't real, but God is. Not only that, but here's some great practical theology in some tiny words: *from*, *for*, and *through*. We all come *from* God the Father, we all exist *for* God the Father, and we were all created *through* Jesus and continue to exist *through* Him. All that matters is Jesus!

Idols are not real. There's no reason to feel guilty if you find yourself eating a McIdol with cheese.

> However, not all possess this knowledge. (1 Cor. 8:7)

Some people just don't know this yet, and the entire question of whether to eat food sacrificed to idols became an ethical struggle for many in the church because of their ignorance.

> But some, through former association with
> idols, eat food as really offered to an idol, and

> their conscience, being weak, is defiled. Food
> will not commend us to God. We are no worse
> off if we do not eat, and no better off if we do.
> (1 Cor. 8:7–8)

Some people in the church used to worship idols. They would take their goat into the temple and watch it get cut into three sections. They would smell the burning flesh of the sacrifice, they would taste the meat at the feast, and they would buy some to take home. Now, as Christians, they knew they couldn't worship the idol anymore, but when they walked by the meat in the marketplace, they felt as though buying it would be encouraging idol worship. They felt that it would be an insult to God and would count as participation in idol worship. Paul reminded them that food didn't change your position in Christ. In fact, Paul said it didn't matter at all. You can walk by the temple and buy the one-third goat your neighbor just sacrificed to an idol. You can go to the Chinese food restaurant with the little temple to Buddha.

But that's not the end of the story.

> But take care that this right of yours does not
> somehow become a stumbling block to the
> weak. For if anyone sees you who have knowl-
> edge eating in an idol's temple, will he not be
> encouraged, if his conscience is weak, to eat
> food offered to idols? And so by your knowledge

this weak person is destroyed, the brother for
whom Christ died. Thus, sinning against your
brothers and wounding their conscience when it
is weak, you sin against Christ. (1 Cor. 8:9–12)

In other words, some people have overactive consciences
because of their lifestyles before becoming Christians. Because of
this, things that are not really sins seem like sins to them. They
feel guilty emotionally even though they are legally not guilty.

When Paul described those with the overactive consciences,
he used the word *weak*. Here are some other words that can be
used instead of *weak*: *powerless, impotent, ill, unsure, immature*.
None of these are good things. And when you are one of these
things, you want to get over it, like the stomach flu.

Weak people are those who are immature in their understanding of the freedoms we have in Christ. They wrestle with the
freedom they have in Christ and they are always feeling guilty,
constantly worried about tripping up and doing something that
God will be displeased with. It's important to remember that
if you are weak, you can't just force yourself not to be weak
anymore. That's like people with the stomach flu trying to force
themselves not to barf or make themselves get up and act as
though they are fine.

In this context, a weak person was someone who freaked out
at the idea of eating food sacrificed to idols.

So two things are true simultaneously. First, if you do
something that causes another to sin against his conscience,

you are in sin because you are "destroying" your brother. That's kind of intense. Second, it is not good to stay weak, and you should encourage your brother to mature in his faith, to "grow up."

Paul knew the Corinthians had specific, weak people they were pouring their lives into. He encouraged them to give up their own freedom for the sake of their brothers and sisters in Christ, but only in very particular instances. This is not about being worried that someone will see you and be "offended" by you or disagree with you in this area. Think about this for a second. Some Christians think drinking any caffeine is wrong. Others think drinking any coffee that is not fair trade is wrong. Some Christians think shopping at Walmart is wrong. Some think watching R-rated movies is wrong. Where does it end?

Paul was writing this passage to the strong, not to the weak. Otherwise, we would have seen him encouraging the weak to become strong.

So let's break this down. Paul says:

Buy whatever meat you want in the market. You are free!

When you go to eat at someone's house, don't question the food the host puts before you. You are free!

But ... if someone else is there and he is worried about eating because he doesn't understand his freedom, don't eat. You are still free, but in this case, love trumps your freedom.

This has a very real impact not just on your own freedom, but on your brother's as well! Because of his weak conscience, he is stuck in step three.

STEP FOUR: FREE (NOT BEING GUILTY AND NOT FEELING GUILTY)

For so many of us, taking this step is difficult, if not altogether elusive. How do we finally get to a place where our experience catches up to our reality? How do we live in the freedom we already have?

We need to begin by viewing our guilt the same way God does. Remember: because of Jesus, you have been set free from the Law, religion, and sin! Satan can't throw that in your face anymore. As Elyse Fitzpatrick said at a conference I attended once, "Since there is no longer a law to disobey, Satan can no longer accuse you of breaking it!"[3]

So how does God view your guilt? It's all over the Bible, practically cover to cover. I'm going to list a bunch of verses for you to read. Take your time and slowly read each one. I mean it. Don't skip this. It's the Word of God. It's God telling you what He thinks of your sin. You may even want to print out these verses and stick them all over the place so you can keep reminding yourself.

> I will forgive their iniquity, and *I will remember their sin no more*. (Jer. 31:34)

> He will again have compassion on us;
>   *he will tread our iniquities underfoot.*

You will *cast all our sins*
    into the depths of the sea. (Mic. 7:19)

I, I am he
    who *blots out your transgressions* for my own
        sake,
    and *I will not remember your sins.*
        (Isa. 43:25)

Therefore, if anyone is in Christ, he is a new creation. The old has passed away; behold, the new has come. All this is from God, who through Christ reconciled us to himself and gave us the ministry of reconciliation; that is, in Christ God was reconciling the world to himself, *not counting their trespasses against them*, and entrusting to us the message of reconciliation. (2 Cor. 5:17–19)

For you are all children of light, children of the day. We are not of the night or of the darkness. (1 Thess. 5:5)

But you are a chosen race, a royal priesthood, a holy nation, a people for his own possession, that you may proclaim the excellencies of him who called you out of darkness into his marvelous light. (1 Pet. 2:9)

See what kind of love the Father has given to us,
that we should be called children of God; and so
we are (1 John 3:1)

The reason for the disconnect between what these verses say
and what we feel is that while we are now *positionally* seated with
Christ in the heavenly places, *conditionally* we are still here on
earth where our sinful flesh continues to do battle with our new
nature. That's why we *feel* guilty even though we *aren't* guilty.

Remember this picture?

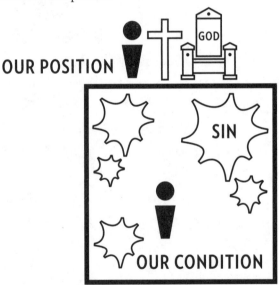

The key to dealing with feelings of condemnation is to remember your position with Jesus in the heavenly places. When you are
feeling condemned, it just shows that every fiber of your being is
longing for the day when your sinful carcass will finally be swallowed

up in your positional righteousness. But that day is in the future: it's far away, and all of us are stuck in the here and now. So when Paul writes in Romans 8:1 that "there is therefore now no condemnation for those who are in Christ Jesus," we give a conflicted nod. Sure, God the Father no longer condemns us in an eternal sense because of the person and work of Jesus, but He certainly must condemn us now (or at least frown every time He thinks about us), right?

Wrong.

Being a pastor of a fairly large church in a pretty small community presents me with opportunities to see this firsthand on a regular basis, because I run into people I know everywhere I go. One night, I was at the bar with some friends. I was on my way to get a drink when I ran into a guy who attends my church. The color drained out of his face, and he quickly said, "I am here to get a sandwich." No "Hello." No "How are you?" Just a stricken "I am here to get a sandwich." To which I replied, "That's nice. I am here to get a beer." He breathed a sigh of relief.

You see, sometimes we carry around this twitchy guilt when really we just need to breathe and remember we have been set free.

I love how Martin Luther put it:

> Whenever the devil harasses you thus, seek the company of men or drink more, or joke and talk nonsense, or do some other merry thing. Sometimes we must drink more, sport, recreate ourselves, aye, and even sin a little to spite the devil, so that we leave him no place for troubling our consciences

with trifles. We are conquered if we try too consci-
entiously not to sin at all. So when the devil says
to you: "Do not drink," answer him: "I will drink,
and right freely, just because you tell me not to."[4]

DISCUSSION QUESTIONS

Do you experience guilt often? If so, how does it affect you? What
do you do with it?

If God's people are Satan's target, what can you expect in your own
life as far as guilt and accusations go? How can knowing this be
encouraging?

Some people think they know God, but they don't. As Titus 1:16
says, a lot of people "profess to know God, but they deny him by
their works." What are some things people do that make them feel as
though they are okay with God? How is it possible for people to feel
as though they know God when in reality they don't?

A conscience can be seared by sin, and eventually right and wrong
begin to taste the same. Discuss some examples of where you've seen
this happen or experienced it yourself.

There is a time in our lives when we come to realize we actually are guilty of sin (see step two) and need a savior. How and when has this happened for you?

Is it hard for you to shake your guilt? Do you know in your head that you're free yet you have a hard time actually accepting that?

"Ignorance does not know that it does not know. True knowledge does not know and knows it." What do you think about this statement? Do you ever have a hard time admitting there are things you don't know?

What does it mean to be "weak" in the context of 1 Corinthians 8?

The author talks about how we may beat ourselves up for things that aren't even sinful. Like the Corinthians who were having a hard time eating food sacrificed to idols, we may have areas in our lives that feel sinful to us because of our past experiences. What are some areas you may struggle in and need more boundaries where someone else may not?

On the flip side, what are some areas where others may struggle where you don't? What does the Bible tell us to do when we are in these situations? Discuss some examples of how this has or could play out for you personally.

When you read through the verses that discuss what God thinks of your sin, what does this tell you? Do these verses change the way you view your own sin or how you view God?

Talk about the Martin Luther quote at the end of this chapter. What do you think he meant by this? Do you agree?

CHAPTER 7

SET FREE *FOR FREEDOM FROM SHAME*

Phil is somewhere in his late forties or early fifties. The first time I met him, he cheerfully bounded up to me as I was pumping gas. He had been attending the church I pastor for a while, and because we never had a chance to meet face to face, he figured the gas station was as good a place as any.

We interacted pleasantly over the following months, and nothing in his demeanor betrayed the sorrowful man I would talk with the next time we met. This time, he didn't bound as he approached. He walked up to me tentatively as if experimenting with a new way to walk (which it turned out he was).

"I am a recovering alcoholic, and the shame of that has hung over my head for seventeen years."

During my sermon that Saturday evening, I reminded the church that I was a "recovering hypocrite" and put everyone on warning that my ailment could rear its ugly head at any moment. I talked about the guilt I struggled with, and then I mentioned, almost as an aside, "For some of you, maybe your issue isn't *guilt* but *shame*." That statement opened up a spot deep inside of Phil he had dutifully been trying to ignore.

He was forgiven. He knew it. His customary cheerfulness was the result of a joy that comes only from Jesus, and that's what most people saw in him. But on the inside, he was ashamed, and shame is easier to hide.

You see, guilt is external; it declares we have *done* something wrong. Shame is internal; it declares, "I *am* something wrong." Often, just like Phil, we can keep the world from seeing our shame as it eats us from the inside out.

I appreciate David Powlison's helpful distinction: "Guilt is an awareness of failure against a standard.... Shame is a sense of failure before the eyes of someone."[1] In a sense, this makes guilt a little easier to pin down and work with—we can see the standard and exactly where we have missed the mark. Shame is a slippery little sucker because it is affected by whoever is watching us. Our propensity to curse like a sailor may go unnoticed when we are watching a game with our friends, but it brings us great shame when hanging with Nana. We may feel a need to cover up the tattoos in the office or refrain from singing along to Justin Bieber at the neighborhood barbecue because intuitively we know the eyes watching us will take us down a notch if we don't.

Now before I roll into this too far, I want to be clear that I am looking at this as a pastor, not as a highly educated psychologist or counselor. In fact, my lack of education is a source of a lot of my own personal shame.

You see, I am a college dropout.

There's a longer story behind that statement, but any attempts to tell it will make it seem as though I am trying to make excuses. The simple fact is, despite my parents' encouragement and financial support, despite all the middle-class opportunities I grew up with, I stopped short of earning my degree. And my lack of a bachelor's degree has kept me from doing any serious graduate work. Several years ago, I had the opportunity to study with some fantastic seminary professors for a year, but all I have to show for it is an unaccredited certificate from a program that doesn't even exist anymore.

Most of the time, I am comfortable with this area of my life, at least on the surface. That is, of course, until I hang out with other pastors. I often find myself spending time with guys who have earned at least one, and often several, advanced degrees. They will casually debate the Bible in Greek (literally, they will debate *in Greek*). In those moments, I am painfully aware that I have to rely on software to translate the Bible's original languages and that my assistant, who is in his first year of seminary, already knows more Greek than I do.

When these conversations with my educated friends take place, I get uncharacteristically quiet. In my shame, I silently plead with God that no one will notice, or worse, that no one will ask me, "Where did you do your seminary work?"

From all outside indications, I have been successful in ministry. I pastor a large, rapidly growing church. I speak at conferences around the world. I even have the cell phone numbers of prominent pastors and leaders. Yet I don't feel like I belong in the club.

I am a college dropout, and I am ashamed.

This is why shame is so hard to deal with. Very few people know this part of my life (unless this book sells well, which will probably just feed my insecurity). Shame is a solitary issue, and many of us, no matter how much we wish we could get rid of the shame, have wrapped it so tightly around our identities that we are afraid that if we lose it, we will lose who we are. We fear that our shame is *all* we are, and we desperately wish it wasn't that way.

Shame is an incredibly lonely place to live.

As followers of Jesus, our shame is often amplified because the eyes that are watching us are God's eyes. Just read these verses and think how terrifying they are for someone stuck in shame:

> The eyes of the LORD are in every place, keeping watch on the evil and the good. (Prov. 15:3)

> For the eyes of the Lord are on the righteous, and his ears are open to their prayer. But the face of the Lord is against those who do evil. (1 Pet. 3:12)

> For the eyes of the LORD run to and fro throughout the whole earth, to give strong support to those whose heart is blameless toward him. You have done foolishly in this, for from now on you will have wars. (2 Chron. 16:9)

To Christians wrestling with shame, these verses can be terrifying because we can just feel God's disappointment in us oozing out of each word. Other people's words toward us and our words toward ourselves get placed in God's mouth, and we are sure that if He had a chance to be really honest with us, He would be the one to say:

"You will never amount to anything."
"You are worthless."
"You are a self-centered jerk."
"You are filthy."
"You really shouldn't be a pastor."

These shameful messages barrage many of us from the time we are very young, and they build into a destructive identity. Because of things we have done (and sometimes because of things done to us), judgments are made on who we are. Over time, these messages burrow themselves deep into our identities, and because we believe what we have been told about ourselves, we feel ashamed.

The beauty of the gospel is that it tells us something completely different about our identities. This is most beautifully shown to us in the very familiar story of Jesus interacting with a woman who was steeped in shame:

[Jesus] left Judea and departed again for Galilee.
And he had to pass through Samaria. So he came

> to a town of Samaria called Sychar, near the field
> that Jacob had given to his son Joseph. Jacob's
> well was there; so Jesus, wearied as he was from
> his journey, was sitting beside the well. It was
> about the sixth hour. (John 4:3–6)

Jesus "had to pass through Samaria." This is an interesting statement by John. It is factually true that the shortest distance between Judea and Galilee was through Samaria; however, most Jews would not take that route because they couldn't stand the people they would have to encounter on the way. Going through Samaria meant dealing with Samaritans, a racially mixed group of people who practiced a form of Judaism that "real Jews" despised. They would rather cross mountains and rivers and add days to their journey rather than run into "those people."

The Samaritans, on the other hand, were probably happy to live their lives and practice their religion without the hassle—that is, until the rare moment when a Jew would pass through their town and the shame of being "the despised other" would well up inside of them again.

In this story, Jesus was that Jew.

> Jesus, wearied as he was from his journey, was
> sitting beside the well. It was about the sixth
> hour. A woman from Samaria came to draw
> water. Jesus said to her, "Give me a drink."
> (John 4:6–7)

In this short passage, we learn a lot about this Samaritan woman and about Jesus. This is a woman with a reason to hide, and it's obvious she wanted to be alone. How do we know this? Because it was "about the sixth hour," which means "about noon." That was a strange time of day to fetch water. Normally, women would go to the well at sunrise or sundown, because it was cooler and carrying water was extremely hard work. They could also spend the time walking back and forth with one another, chit-chatting about daily life.

The woman in this story avoided all of that by going at the one time of day she wasn't going to run into anyone; she went at high noon, near the peak of the heat. We find out later in this chapter that this was four months until the harvest season, so it was also one of the hottest times of the year. Simply put, she went to the well to do the grueling work of hauling water at one of the worst times of the day.

Nobody does that without a good reason. It gets stranger when you consider where this well was located. All the wells in Sychar were situated outside of the city walls, and historians tell us the well she chose was about half a mile from the city.[2] To get there, she would likely have had to pass by several other perfectly good wells.

This whole thing isn't adding up.

She went at this odd hour to this inconvenient well to avoid people. It's clear she wanted to be alone.

But there was also something special about this particular well. It was Jacob's well. It had spiritual significance to Jews and Samaritans alike.[3] We come to find out that, despite her shame, she was a spiritually interested person. I wonder if being alone at that special well gave her comfort as well as time to think and pray.

But on that day, she arrived at the well to see the last person a Samaritan woman who desired to be left alone wanted to see: a Jewish man.

Great.

And then He asked for water.

Even better.

> The Samaritan woman said to him, "How is it that you, a Jew, ask for a drink from me, a woman of Samaria?" (For Jews have no dealings with Samaritans.) Jesus answered her, "If you knew the gift of God, and who it is that is saying to you, 'Give me a drink,' you would have asked him, and he would have given you living water."
> (John 4:9–10)

This turned into a little debate about what "living water" was, with her likely confusing it for some sort of indoor plumbing. "The woman said to him, 'Sir, give me this water, so that I will not be thirsty or have to come here to draw water'" (John 4:15).

You can see her countenance perk up a little bit with the far-off hope of never having to leave her house again.

Up to this point, while she had bristled with her racial shame, she had been able to hide her personal shame. That is, until Jesus decided to go there.

> Jesus said to her, "Go, call your husband, and come
> here." The woman answered him, "I have no hus-
> band." Jesus said to her, "You are right in saying, 'I
> have no husband'; for you have had five husbands,
> and the one you now have is not your husband.
> What you have said is true." (John 4:16–18)

Oh, snap.

You see, people who are living in the "shame cycle" don't like
to tell the truth, or if their secret is about to come to light, they like
to hide behind half truths. For years, I was the master of "I *went to*
Michigan State." When asked what my degree was in, a quick "I
studied history" would usually get me off the hook.

The Samaritan woman was able to dodge Jesus's inquiry the
same way: "I have no husband." Her statement was technically
true—with a dash of "Please don't dig any further." But Jesus loved
her too much to let it go, so He called her out on all of it. Five
ex-husbands, living with her lover—it was all on the table. Her
shame was exposed.

No wonder she went to the well at noon! She was hoping
to avoid the women of her small community (who likely looked
down on her) and, more importantly, the men (who likely knew
she had "been around the block"). She had been trapped in the
shame cycle, and with a fifteen-second statement, Jesus brought
everything into the light.

Lots of ink has been spilled trying to figure out how to break
someone out of shame, but here's the one-word Bible answer: Jesus.

You can't do it without Him because you are like a dog chained to a post in the middle of the yard. All you can do is run around in a circle.

But when Jesus sets you free from the chain, you can leave the circle behind too. That's what He did for this woman. Of course, she initially saw him as a Jewish man who disapproved of her, didn't understand what she'd been through, and wanted something from her, but that was because she didn't know He was on a mission. She didn't know Jesus "had to pass through Samaria" to find her at the well. She didn't know He was more than just a random Jewish man passing through town but that He was, in fact, the Jewish Messiah her people were longing for. She didn't know that He was the God of Jacob or that He was the one Jacob's life pointed toward. And she certainly didn't know He was about to break her out of the shame cycle. But to break her out, He had to confront her with her sin. Only then would she find what she was longing for.

In her shame, she was trying to hide her sin, but Jesus said to her, "I know your sin. I know *you*." People who are living with shame don't want to be known. They don't want to be exposed. But Jesus sees us, even in our deepest, darkest, smelliest places, and He exposes our sins for what they are. Only then can the cycle be broken. Of course, this woman responded the same way many of us do—by changing the topic.

> The woman said to him, "Sir, I perceive that
> you are a prophet. Our fathers worshiped on

> this mountain, but you say that in Jerusalem
> is the place where people ought to worship."
> (John 4:19–20)

To get the attention off herself, she tried to start an argument about religion, but that exposed a crack in her armor. You see, Samaritans believed that, after Moses, there would be no more prophets until the Messiah came.

So why did she call Jesus a prophet? Perhaps she was beginning to put some pieces together—and Jesus added more to the picture.

> Jesus said to her, "Woman, believe me, the hour
> is coming when neither on this mountain nor
> in Jerusalem will you worship the Father. You
> worship what you do not know; we worship
> what we know, for salvation is from the Jews.
> But the hour is coming, and is now here, when
> the true worshipers will worship the Father in
> spirit and truth, for the Father is seeking such
> people to worship him. God is spirit, and those
> who worship him must worship in spirit and
> truth." (John 4:21–24)

These ideas pointed toward the next prophet to come after Moses: the Messiah. She responded by making a statement that was really a question in disguise:

> The woman said to him, "I know that Messiah
> is coming (he who is called Christ). When he
> comes, he will tell us all things." (John 4:25)

Can you sense her tentative hope? I imagine a moment of silence passed here. She had just dropped a big hint (was Jesus the Messiah?), and she was waiting for a bite. Jesus bit.

> "I who speak to you am he." (John 4:26)

Look at the trajectory of this conversation! For her to accept who Jesus was, she needed to first accept the truth about who she was. The painful truth about her sin and the painful truth about her shame had to be brought into the open.

The result of this encounter was a clean break from her shame cycle.

> So the woman left her water jar and went away
> into town and said to the people, "Come, see a
> man who told me all that I ever did. Can this be
> the Christ?" They went out of the town and were
> coming to him. (John 4:28–30)

"Come, see a man who told me all that I ever did."
Remarkable.
Just the other side of noon, this woman was in hiding because of all she ever did. She went through extraordinary pains to make

sure her past wasn't the center of anyone's conversation (especially if she was within earshot). And now? Now, the centerpiece of her declaration to the entire village, the conversation starter she led off with, was the *former* source of her shame: "Come, see a man who told me all that I ever did."

This woman, who started her day wanting nothing but to be left alone, became the voice of salvation to her entire town, and they flocked to Jesus. The women she was avoiding, her ex-husbands, her lover, all of them came to meet the savior who had changed this woman in one radical encounter.

This same Jesus wants to set you free from your shame too. And the truth is, if you are in Christ, you are already set free. You just don't know it. To worship Jesus in spirit and in truth is not only to accept the truth of who *He* is but also to accept the truth of who *He says you are now in Him*! The Bible is jam-packed with descriptions of who you are in Christ. A few that deal with our shame tell us we are chosen, we are the righteousness of God, we are new creations, we are children of God, we are forgiven and redeemed, and we are chained to God so tightly that nothing can rip us from His hand.

This is what you *are* in Christ:

You are *chosen*.

> Even as he chose us in him before the foundation of the world, that we should be holy and blameless before him. (Eph. 1:4)

We all want to be picked for something great, but if elementary school dodge ball has taught us anything, our selection is based on performance. In a sense, our being chosen for salvation is based on performance as well. Only it's not our own performance—it's Jesus's!

You are the *righteousness of God.*

> For our sake he made him to be sin who knew no sin, so that in him we might become the righteousness of God. (2 Cor. 5:21)

Jesus's performance was so flawless on earth that when you are picked for His team, it can be said of you, "You are righteousness." In your new position, you are now the definition of all that is right and good in the world. How can this be?

You are a *new creation.*

> Therefore, if anyone is in Christ, he is a new creation. The old has passed away; behold, the new has come. (2 Cor. 5:17)

God created humankind perfect once, and He can do it again. The proof is you. You aren't the old you; you aren't even some sort of incremental upgrade. You are brand spanking new.

You are a *child of God*.

> For in Christ Jesus you are all sons of God, through
> faith. (Gal. 3:26)

> For you are all children of light, children of the
> day. We are not of the night or of the darkness.
> (1 Thess. 5:5)

We discussed this in chapter 4. But let's remind ourselves
again: we are beloved children of the King and children of light.
Nothing will ever change our place in God's family.

You are *forgiven* and *redeemed*.

> In him we have redemption through his blood,
> the forgiveness of our trespasses, according to the
> riches of his grace. (Eph. 1:7)

What a wonderful truth. According to God's riches, which
He measures in grace, you were purchased by the most precious
currency in the world: Jesus's blood. The amount He paid was so
staggeringly high that it—once for all time—paid off any debt you
owed or ever could rack up in a billion lifetimes.

You are a *royal priest*.

> But you are a chosen race, a royal priesthood, a
> holy nation, a people for his own possession, that
> you may proclaim the excellencies of him who
> called you out of darkness into his marvelous
> light. (1 Pet. 2:9)

Have you ever had a moment when you were listening to a pastor preach who said something almost as an aside but it stopped you dead in your tracks? That happened to me recently as I was listening to Stephen Um from Citylife Presbyterian Church in Boston. The comment he made was brilliant in its simplicity: "The opposite of shame is dignity."[4]

Dignity. That's what Jesus offers every single one of His followers. Dignity is something worthy of honor or respect. When Jesus unchains us from our sin, He places us with Him in the place of greatest honor in the universe: with Him at the right hand of God the Father. From that place of honor, He gives us a job as a royal priest, proclaiming His excellencies to a world in need of a savior.

It doesn't matter if we are the CEO of a Fortune 500 company or a homeless person trying to find our next meal, in God's eyes we have dignity, honor, and respect through Jesus our King.

You are *chained* to God so tightly, nothing can rip you from His hand.

> For I am sure that neither death nor life, nor
> angels nor rulers, nor things present nor things

> to come, nor powers, nor height nor depth, nor
> anything else in all creation, will be able to sepa-
> rate us from the love of God in Christ Jesus our
> Lord. (Rom. 8:38–39)

Remember this verse? It reminds us that no matter what our *condition*, our *position* is with Jesus, seated at the right hand of God the Father. You have been unchained from the Law, religion, sin, guilt, and shame—but that's not all! You have been chained to Jesus, and that chain will never break.

Nothing in all of creation (yourself included) can ever pull you away from God. You don't have to worry that your sin or someone else's sin can do you in. From an eternal perspective, you are forever locked in to your relationship with God.

When you put all of this together, you can be confident that, because of Jesus, you are a new creation: a forgiven, redeemed child of the King, the chosen righteousness of God who is so connected to Him you can never be ripped away. Like the woman at the well, the source of your shame has been taken away, and you have been set free!

Because of this new freedom, you now have a new calling on your life too.

You are *called* to a *holy calling*, to be a *saint*.

> God, who saved us and called us to a holy calling,
> not because of our works but because of his own

purpose and grace, which he gave us in Christ
Jesus before the ages began. (2 Tim. 1:8–9)

To those sanctified in Christ Jesus, called to be
saints together with all those who in every place
call upon the name of our Lord Jesus Christ, both
their Lord and ours. (1 Cor. 1:2)

When the woman at the well was set free from her shame, it led to
an entire town's conversion. She couldn't take any credit for it. In fact,
you could say that the only thing she contributed was the very thing
that sent her into hiding. My story is similar. The path to my writing
this book, which includes the church I pastor, is inextricably linked
to my dropping out of school. You see, part of the reason I quit was
because I wanted to transfer to Bible school to eventually go into the
ministry. My wife had another couple of years of school, so I picked
up a full-time job until she finished. We also began to volunteer more
at our church—both to serve and to gain some much-needed ministry experience. That volunteer work led to a job. Fast-forward more
than twenty years, and I have never left that church. If I had stayed in
school, it's quite possible none of that would have happened.

The very thing I am ashamed of is the very thing Jesus has used
for the Father's glory in my life. Like the woman at the well, I am
frequently tempted to think I *am* something wrong. But nothing
could be further from the truth. When God looks at me, He sees
the dignity that His Son, Jesus, purchased for me on the cross.

That means, in the only way that truly matters, *I am something right*.

I am a chosen, forgiven, redeemed, righteous, new creation—a child of the King, secure for all eternity. And if you are in Christ, you are too.

So is Phil, the man who talked with me after the Saturday-night service a few months ago. After sharing with me the shame he had carried for seventeen years over his alcoholism, he thanked me for the message and walked out the door. The next morning, as I was preparing to give the same message again, he walked by me (a little steadier than he had the night before), placed his hand gently on my shoulder on the way, then sat down to listen to the truth again. That's what we need. We need to hear God's truth on this again and again and again.

I didn't see Phil walk back out of the church after hearing the message a second time, but I suspect that, when he did, he had his head held high.

DISCUSSION QUESTIONS

Some people struggle with guilt, while others may struggle more with shame. Guilt is external (I've done something wrong), while shame is internal (I am something wrong). Which one is more of a struggle for you?

The author shares how not having his college degree can sometimes be a source of shame for him. What are some things in your life that cause you to feel ashamed? What are the messages you have believed about these things in the past or you may be believing today?

The story of Jesus and the woman at the well (John 4) shows us that Jesus reaches out to those buried in shame in order to lift them out of it. The woman at the well was hiding, just like many people struggling with shame do. What did Jesus do to reveal truth to her? What are some similar ways that followers of Christ can reach out to people struggling with shame?

"To worship Jesus in spirit and in truth is not only to accept the truth of who *He* is but also to accept the truth of who *He says you are now in Him*!" Do you accept Jesus in this way? If so, how have you gotten to this point? If not, how can you make it to this state?

When God looks at you, what does He see? How has your church background, family, or culture influenced your thoughts on what you *think* God sees when He looks at you? What does the Bible say God *actually* sees?

The opposite of shame is dignity. And every follower of Jesus is offered dignity. No matter what our job is here on earth, God has given us another job, rich in dignity and responsibility. What is this job He has given us? How does this play out in your life?

Do you believe that nothing—even you yourself—can take you away from God?

In Christ you are chosen. You are the righteousness of God. You are a new creation. You are a child of God. You are forgiven and redeemed. You are a royal priest. You are chained to God so tightly, nothing can rip you from His hand. You are called to a holy calling, to be a saint. Is it hard to believe any of these truths about yourself? Is any one of these particularly hard for you to trust as being true? Discuss which one(s) and why it may be harder to accept some over others.

CHAPTER 8

SET FREE *FOR FREEDOM TO SAY YES*

It is quite possible that you are frustrated with me by now, especially if you are one of those people who likes to get stuff done. If that describes you, I have to warn you that you will likely have a love-hate relationship with this chapter. While this is one of the most practical sections of the whole book, I'm still going to work hard to make sure I don't pile any more chains back onto your weary soul.

I just don't want you to turn out like my friend Rob, who used to be the college pastor at our church. Canadian born, Rob is a former hockey player and looks every bit the part at a hulking six feet, five inches tall. As a way to both stay connected to his favorite sport and create gospel opportunities, he coached the club hockey team at Michigan State University and would often take groups of students to Munn Ice Arena on campus to play broomball. This sport is really just poor man's hockey, replacing the stick with a broom, the puck with a ball, and skates with whatever shoes you want to wear. Throughout all of these activities, Rob would proudly wear his coach's jacket emblazoned with his name across the front: "Coach Rob."

One day, Rob was hosting a birthday party for a bunch of little kids and he was teaching them how to come to a complete stop on the ice. After one demonstration, he was standing there, talking with the kids. He was standing. He wasn't sliding around; he wasn't skating around. He was literally just standing there.

And then he wasn't.

Rob fell.

Rob fell hard.

His head, which had more than six feet to accelerate, slammed into the ice with a loud *bang* that reverberated around the arena. It was apparent, from the incoherent stream of words coming from his mouth, that Rob had suffered a concussion; so a few of his friends quickly rushed him to the hospital. As they sped to the emergency room, Rob wasn't concerned about the throbbing pain in his head or the poking and prodding he was about to endure. All Rob was concerned about was his prized "Coach Rob" jacket; he didn't want anyone to see it. In fact, he was willing to go without any coat at all in the bitter cold Michigan winter because he was embarrassed that someone would find out this hockey coach couldn't stand on the ice.

If we aren't careful, we all have the potential to be Rob.

In this chapter, we are going to have to tread very carefully lest we come crashing down on the ice. On the next few pages, we are going to talk about stepping out onto the ice of obedience. If we don't handle this well, we run the risk of dismantling everything we have built so far in this book. When we start talking about obedience, we can very easily place ourselves back in chains. We can start to fret about our sin, drive ourselves crazy trying to keep the Law, and build monumental false religions that distort Christianity's core message of forgiveness and grace.

Counterintuitively, trying to obey God isn't even the biggest danger. The real threat to our faith is when we actually succeed in obeying.

Now go back and reread those two sentences if you wish, but don't get hung up there because we're going to unpack them in the rest of this chapter.

You see, it's in the moments when we actually get stuff right in our lives that we run the risk of stealing Jesus's glory and begin to take the credit He alone deserves. Our obedience leads to pride, and pride leads to a fall (Prov. 16:18). So as we begin to consider what it means to obey, let's remember the words of the apostle Paul, who said, "Let anyone who thinks that he stands take heed lest he fall" (1 Cor. 10:12).

That's the danger when we have too much confidence in our standing: we fall. And then we slide back into guilt and shame.

With this warning fully locked in, let's talk about obedience.

SORTING OUT OBEDIENCE

As we have already seen, a follower of Jesus is set free from the Law. I don't know about you, but that feels like only a temporary relief to me. While it can be staggering to try to wrap my head around the 613 laws in the Old Testament, I flip over to the New Testament, and it seems as though I am right back at it, staring at over one thousand similar statements in the familiar forms of "do this" and "don't do that." It's tricky because these commands aren't neatly codified as the Law is, and not all of them seem to be for us, since some are given directly to a specific person or group. But make no mistake about it: it's clear that the New Testament of the Bible tells followers of Jesus to do and not to do a whole lot of stuff.

Obedience is clearly a part of the Christian faith. And here's the big question: What is the *purpose* of obedience for a follower of Jesus?

There are a lot of decent answers, but I think they all boil down to one: Our obedience shows the world that we have said yes to Jesus. Since God the Father already sees us like Jesus, we should live in such a way that everyone else does too.

The world really, really needs to see what Jesus looks like.

Over the span of human history, sin seems to have exacted a steep escalating toll on our world. Wars, racial tensions, ethnic divides, abuse of authority (which fuels disrespect of authority), pervasive sexual immorality, materialism, greed, and on and on. In short, there is an increasing sense of open defiance, not just against human laws, but also against God's laws—and even basic human decency.

Wickedness is trampling goodness all around the world.

This great evil starts with every small child. Contrary to what Sarah McLachlan would have you believe, we are not born innocent.[1] Babies and toddlers are the very definition of guilty! Shopping malls and church lobbies are filled with parents trying to move their children from lawlessness to obedience, but it's not an easy switch to flip. To tackle this seemingly insurmountable task, frazzled moms and dads resort to various strategies:

> **Reward:** "If you obey, you get a lollipop."
> **Duty:** "You will obey because I said so!"
> **Fear:** "You will obey or you will get a spanking (or, even worse, you will lose your screen time)!"

Because these are the systems we use to control the lawlessness of little people, they become the same systems we try to use with big people too.

> **Reward:** "If you go to college, you'll get a better paying job!"
> **Duty:** "I will have sex with my husband because I have to."
> **Fear:** "If I don't up my game at work, I will lose my job."

Despite being fairly powerful motivators (that's why they are still in use), none of these methods is ultimately 100 percent successful. Why? Because every conflict includes the battle of at least two sinful wills. More than that, there's additional conflict over what constitutes an appropriate reward, a fair duty, and a level of fear that doesn't create mutiny. It's no wonder that when you throw seven billion people into this sinful system things get tricky.

To make matters worse, in the Christian faith we try to use the same strategies to motivate obedience to God.

> **Reward:** "If you obey God, you'll get material wealth here on earth and a big ol' mansion up in the sky!"
>
> **Duty:** "You have to obey God because it's what He expects of you and you don't want to disappoint Him!"
>
> **Fear:** "If you don't obey God, you will lose your salvation and end up in hell!"

Each of these is a powerful motivator, despite being imprecise at best or theologically inaccurate at worst. Besides being poor methods of behavior modification, none of them truly shows the world why we say yes to Jesus.

The apostle John does a good job showing us how to navigate this in his crazy, nonlinear book of 1 John. In the third chapter, he writes:

> Everyone who makes a practice of sinning also practices lawlessness; sin is lawlessness. You know that he appeared in order to take away sins, and in him there is no sin. (vv. 4–5)

We know that the reason Jesus came to earth and went to the cross was to deal with wickedness and sin. Yes, He was a great teacher; yes, He stood for social justice. But ultimately, He came to deal with sin. His work on the cross served to pay the penalty for sin, and His resurrection from the dead conquered sin's hold. Because all of this is true, John can appropriately say:

> No one who abides in him keeps on sinning; no one who keeps on sinning has either seen him or known him. Little children, let no one deceive you. Whoever practices righteousness is righteous, as he is righteous. Whoever makes a practice of sinning is of the devil, for the devil has been sinning from the beginning. The reason the Son of God appeared was to destroy the works of the devil. No one born of God makes a practice of sinning, for God's seed abides in him; and he cannot keep on sinning, because he has been born of God. By this it is evident who are the children of God, and who are the children of the devil: whoever does not practice righteousness is not of God, nor is the one who does not love his brother. (1 John 3:6–10)

This is a difficult passage to interpret, much less digest. According to the late Ray Stedman, there are at least seven common interpretations, and each provides a wildly different application.[2] Let's look quickly at all of them to see what we are dealing with.

Option 1: Once you become a Christian, you cannot commit even one single sin. Of course, John pretty much rules this one out in the first chapter of 1 John when he states clearly, "If we say we have no sin, we deceive ourselves" (v. 8). When you look at pretty much every Christian in the Bible and every Christian you have ever met, you know this option doesn't hold water.

Option 2: Sin is really narrow and only things such as murder count. The Bible never makes that distinction, so that is clearly too far to go. This option just makes people feel better about their favorite little sins.

Option 3: This passage is talking about deliberate sins. In other words, if you accidentally sin you are fine because, you know, it was an accident and all. But, of course, we have all deliberately sinned after becoming Christians, so this can't be what this passage is saying.

Option 4: If Christians sin, it's not really a sin anymore because Jesus has saved them from their sins. This one is just strange. It does nothing more than provide a loosely veiled justification for sin by redefining sin as something a Christian can't commit. Besides providing a convenient philosophical loophole, it is really an offense to Jesus and His work on the cross by saying sin is no longer that big of a deal.

Option 5: John is painting the picture of an ideal world, but it's really not possible. Besides the fact that John doesn't say that (at all), it would defeat the entire case he is building and would flatly contradict his thesis statement: "I am writing these things to you so that you may not sin" (1 John 2:1). If it weren't possible, John wouldn't have written this letter.

Option 6: As Christians, we have two natures now, and our new nature cannot sin. This is actually a fairly decent option that would be pretty consistent with Scripture. It is our old nature that sinned before we became a Christian and that continues to sin now. Unfortunately, this interpretation seems to imply that either there is no way to grow in your faith as a Christian or John was taking lots of time making a case for something we can't do anything about.

Option 7: A Christian will not (and therefore, cannot) forever continue in a pattern of unrepentant sin. This is where I land—and it's no big surprise that I'd put the interpretation I agree with last, right? Of course, we will need to take some time fleshing this one out (pun intended). The battle between our flesh and spirit is ongoing (Gal. 5:17), and it is precisely that: a battle. Sometimes one side is winning; sometimes the other side is. You can go read about the apostle Paul's own battle with sin in Romans 7. But Christians, filled with the Holy Spirit, will always ultimately know that our sin is sin. There may be a season when we ignore God, when our consciences are seared, when we do whatever we want, but eventually, the Holy Spirit will break through. We have, as this passage says, been reborn. Over the course of our lives, God's light will shine on new nooks and crannies of our lives that need to be dealt with. No, we will never be free from sin during this life, but we will grow more and more into the likeness of Jesus. We can't help it.

There is no scriptural guarantee that our spiritual growth will be a fast process, and that is frustrating because we live in a microwave culture. We cook our burritos in less than a minute, receive our online purchases in a single day (and, I suspect, via rocket-propelled drone delivery by the time this book comes out), and get loan approval in fifteen minutes—guaranteed!

Then we come to our spiritual lives and our growth is sometimes so slow it makes a *turtle* look like it's moving at the speed of a rocket-propelled drone. The new Christians I have met who *seem* to mature quickly (on the outside, anyway) are those who had things pretty well together before they came to Christ. They were nice and generally moral people. I don't, by any means, intend to imply that their sin wasn't damning, or their conversion real. It's just that their outward change doesn't always seem as radical as some of the more "outwardly" jacked-up people I have seen come to Christ.

Whenever we do baptisms at our church, we record testimony videos of those taking the plunge. It is hard for me to keep it together as I hear people tell stories of their changed lives. Often the contrast is striking, as the video cuts from someone who grew up as a generally "good person" but recently realized that wasn't going to be enough to be right with God, to a dude who got stabbed a bunch of times in prison, became a Christian, then went back to prison, tried to get his life together, and can barely remember not to use profanity in a video made for church.

We would look at these two and immediately jump to the conclusion that the first person was "more mature in the faith," when it was quite possible the second person was growing faster and showing more fruit in his life.

Sometimes it's good to remember that Jesus gives the same reward to everyone, isn't it?

Remember the provocative parable of the laborers in the vineyard of Matthew 20:1–16? Oh, it's a good one. A landowner promises to pay a particular wage to some guys in exchange for doing some work for him. As the day progresses, more people are added to the workforce, and they are each offered the exact same amount. At the end of the day, the guys who worked the whole day were ticked! Why should they be paid the same amount as the guys who worked just one stinking hour? The boss's reply is stunningly true, if seemingly unfair:

> "Am I not allowed to do what I choose with what belongs to me? Or do you begrudge my generosity?" So the last will be first, and the first last. (Matt. 20:15–16)

The wonderful truth of the gospel is that this is not your work. It is God's! As Paul declared to the Philippians, "I am sure of this, that he who began a good work in you will bring it to completion at the day of Jesus Christ" (Phil. 1:6).

This is an astonishing relief! While it is true that Christians will not continue in a pattern of unrepentant sin forever, the work of making this happen is not ours to do. We are not in the completing business. God is.

So here's the big question I am asked all the time: If this is true, how can I *know* that I am saved? From a spiritual perspective, how do I know what team I am playing for?

TEAM JESUS OR TEAM SATAN

> Little children, let no one deceive you. Whoever practices righteousness is righteous, as he is righteous. Whoever makes a practice of sinning is of the devil, for the devil has been sinning from the beginning. The reason the Son of God appeared was to destroy the works of the devil. (1 John 3:7–8)

In this passage, John laid out an either-or scenario; it's one or the other. We are either God's kids or the devil's kids. The way we know which team we are playing for is by watching how we play the game. Our character is the evidence of our team.

One of the clearest descriptions of the devil's nature is in the Old Testament book of Isaiah:

> How you are fallen from heaven,
>   O Day Star, son of Dawn!
> How you are cut down to the ground,
>   you who laid the nations low!
> You said in your heart,
>   "I will ascend to heaven;

above the stars of God
    I will set my throne on high;
I will sit on the mount of assembly
    in the far reaches of the north;
I will ascend above the heights of the clouds;
    I will make myself like the Most High."
        (14:12–14)

Do you see the key issue here? The devil refused to *abide in God*; instead, he wanted to *take the place of God*. "I will, I will, I will, I will." When this world is all about the almighty Me, when we want to make ourselves into God, we are playing for "Team Devil." On the flip side, when we *abide in Jesus*, it will also be evident. In John 15, Jesus said this:

> Abide in me, and I in you. As the branch cannot bear fruit by itself, unless it abides in the vine, neither can you, unless you abide in me. I am the vine; you are the branches. Whoever abides in me and I in him, he it is that bears much fruit, for apart from me you can do nothing. If anyone does not abide in me he is thrown away like a branch and withers; and the branches are gathered, thrown into the fire, and burned. If you abide in me, and my words abide in you, ask whatever you wish, and it will be done for you. By this my Father is glorified, that you

bear much fruit and so prove to be my disciples.
(John 15:4–8)

Jesus is very clear. How will people know you belong to Him?
Fruit.

What is fruit? Obedience.

Where does fruit (obedience) come from? Jesus.

Can you bear fruit (obey) without Him? No.

Instead of remembering our *position* in Christ, we too often
fret about our *condition* and try to generate fruit from the wrong
place. Or worse, we try to zip-tie fresh fruit to a dead tree and
think we are fooling everyone around us. But the fruit of a changed
life comes from a new life in Jesus, not from our silly attempts to
look more righteous.

The most famous passage about what this new fruit looks like
is Galatians 5:22–23:

> But the fruit of the Spirit is love, joy, peace,
> patience, kindness, goodness, faithfulness, gen-
> tleness, self-control; against such things there is
> no law.

Now the order Jesus lays out is vitally important. You abide in
(belong to) Jesus first, then comes obedience. That means that, if
you belong to Jesus, the fruit *will* appear—in a very real sense, you
can't help it. In fact, the Greek word for *fruit* is singular. It's not
as though Paul is rattling off isolated qualities you have to develop

in your life. Rather, he is describing the one fruit of a changed life that God is developing in you, regardless if you realize it.

Now let's loop back to 1 John and back up to the second chapter (I warned you John was nonlinear).

> And by this we know that we have come to know him, if we keep his commandments. Whoever says "I know him" but does not keep his commandments is a liar, and the truth is not in him, but whoever keeps his word, in him truly the love of God is perfected. By this we may know that we are in him: whoever says he abides in him ought to walk in the same way in which he walked. (1 John 2:3–6)

Again, do you see the order? If you want to know that you know Jesus (in a saving way), look for fruit. You can say you know Him all you want, but if there is no fruit …

Let me put it this way. You may want to do the right thing by the force of your own will, but you can't. You can try to treat the Christian life like parenting:

> **Reward:** "If I obey, God will let me into heaven."
> **Duty:** "If I obey, it's because I have to."
> **Fear:** "If I obey, I will not go to hell."

But Jesus flips this thing on its head. Obedience comes from knowing Him, and you can know you know Him because you obey. This is how I like to say it: I know, therefore, I obey; I obey, therefore, I know that I know.

You might need to wrestle with the first part of that equation, or maybe you need to wrestle more with the second. You see, the first answers the whole "Now that I'm a Christian, I can do whatever I want" attitude, and the second part answers the question "Am I really a Christian?" Both of these find their answer in the gospel of Jesus.

YOU KNOW, THEREFORE, YOU OBEY (OR OBEDIENCE COMES FROM KNOWING)

"Know" in this sense is having placed your faith in Jesus—in other words, being a Christian. When that happens, obedience naturally follows. It isn't easy, and it isn't fast, but it's natural. Grapes come from a vine. They just do. Yes, you can cultivate that vine and add some water and fertilizer; those are all great things. But without the vine, you have nothing. In the same sense, the Bible is filled with all kinds of practical wisdom on water and fertilizer for your spiritual walk. Reading the Word, prayer, community—stuff like that. But don't mistake the plant food for the plant.

So many people struggle with "knowing" whether they are a Christian. They wonder, *Do I really know Him?* Just asking that question is a good sign. It shows the struggle you have with obedience, and it shows that you—yes, you—*know*.

Make no mistake about it: the standard for a follower of Jesus is high. Look what John said:

> By this we may know that we are in him: whoever
> says he abides in him ought to walk in the same
> way in which [Jesus] walked. (1 John 2:5–6)

Jesus is our savior and our example!
That means the life of a Christian is a life of saying yes to Jesus.
Here's part of our motivation:

> And now, little children, abide in him, so that when
> he appears we may have confidence and not shrink
> from him in shame at his coming. (1 John 2:28)

One of the most frequently mentioned truths in the New Testament is that Jesus is returning (e.g., Heb. 9:28). We will all, regardless if we are Christian, see Jesus. On that day, whether it appears in ten thousand years or before you finish reading this chapter, Jesus is coming back, and some of us may find that we "shrink from him in shame."

What does that mean?

Don't forget John was writing to Christians who were already *positionally* outside of the box. With this statement, he was echoing the words of Paul in 1 and 2 Corinthians (1 Cor. 3:12–15, 4:5; 2 Cor. 5:8). When Jesus returns, it will not be about judgment (for followers of Jesus, we are set free from eternal judgment), but for an evaluation of how we lived our lives on mission for Him here on earth. Did we value what He values, did we leverage all that we had in our lives for His sake, did we take sin seriously?

YOU OBEY, THEREFORE, YOU KNOW THAT YOU KNOW (OR YOU KNOW YOU KNOW BECAUSE YOU OBEY)

When we obey (against even our own will), it is evidence that we play for "Team Jesus." Unfortunately, knowing this can cause us to go into "WebMD mode" in our spiritual lives. You know what that is, right? That's when you begin to encounter some symptoms in your life (like a runny nose or a dull ache), and instead of going to the doctor, you turn to WebMD to diagnose yourself. A few clicks later, and you are convinced your organs are failing. Next thing you know, you start updating your will and gathering your family and friends together to say good-bye. We do the same thing with our spiritual health. Because we know that obedience (or fruit) in our lives is an indicator of our faith, we can place unreasonable expectations on how much fruit we should be seeing.

Each and every time we stumble, we diagnose ourselves and fret about whether we are really saved. But remember, obedience can be a slow grind sometimes. As Matt Chandler once said, "It's a good thing God celebrates limping obedience."[3] If Jesus has set us free and we are doing our best to say yes to Him, we can at least be confident we are limping in the right direction. That's probably why the apostle John doesn't stop with his words about Jesus coming back and how some will shrink in shame. He continues his train of thought by reminding us:

> Beloved, we are God's children now, and what
> we will be has not yet appeared; but we know

that when he appears we shall be like him,
because we shall see him as he is. And everyone
who thus hopes in him purifies himself as he is
pure. (1 John 3:2–3)

To encourage us in our spiritual progress, John tells us two
things about our present, two things about our future, and one
thing about where our hope lies.

In the present:

> "We are God's children *now*." That means you
> are seated with Jesus. So, when you fail to obey,
> don't panic. Your eternity is secure. Yes, your life
> is a mess sometimes now, but the truth of the
> matter is …

> "What we will be has not yet appeared." God is at
> work in you—it's a promise! If you are in Christ,
> He is going to keep working on you day after day
> your whole life. Who you are now is not who you
> will be when He is done.

In the future:

> "We know that when he appears …" Jesus is
> coming back, and on that day, you shall be like

Him. It's a done deal! God is conforming you into the likeness of His Son. It's going to happen, and it is happening. One day in the future, your sin will no longer have a single ounce of control over you. Jesus wins, sin loses, period.

"We shall see him as he is." On that day when you are fully like Jesus, perfect and spotless, you will finally be able to understand fully who He is and what He has done for you. This is what you should hang your hopes on. This is how you fight lawlessness and wickedness in your heart. It's never about what you do. It's always about what Jesus has done and what He will do.

Where our hope lies:

This all means we shouldn't hope in anyone or anything else (ourselves included); we hope in Jesus alone. With our hope squarely in the right place, we can finally face the dos and don'ts in Scripture.

DON'T DO THE *DON'TS*

I've noticed that when it comes to our obedience, we don't have a performance issue—we have an emphasis issue. Too many of us try to live out our Christian faith by focusing on the *don'ts*. Now, don't get me wrong, the *don'ts* are very important. We should never downplay them—just as we should never downplay the Law. It's good to know the standard that God has for us and what sin looks like.

But I want to make a case for a different way of approaching these commands that helps us live out our freedom.

GO ON A *DO* HUNT

Instead of focusing on the *don'ts* in Scripture, focus on the *dos*. Confident in our position and identity in Christ, trusting the Holy Spirit's work in our lives, we simply *live* saying yes to Jesus.

By the way, this isn't some crazy idea I came up with on my own. Jesus, when painting a mental picture of the kingdom of God for the Jews who were looking for a messiah, made this mind-numbing statement:

> You therefore must be perfect, as your heavenly
> Father is perfect. (Matt. 5:48)

Great. Here it comes, right? The guilt and shame are already lurking on the edges of our minds. Then, in the very next verse, he said:

> Beware of practicing your righteousness before
> other people in order to be seen by them, for then

> you will have no reward from your Father who is
> in heaven. (Matt. 6:1)

So, wait. If I am reading this right, I'm supposed to be perfect (which is impossible), but I'm also supposed to make sure no one notices when I actually get something right! Why is Jesus always messing with my head? Jesus then gets into a whole lot of *dos* and *don'ts* in the remainder of the chapter, and you can almost feel the tension rising up in His hearers—it definitely has that result on me!

The type of life Jesus is describing seems infinitely out of reach.

It seems appropriate that at this point, Jesus then transitions to talking about anxiety, urging His disciples, "Do not be anxious" (Matt. 6:31), even about simple stuff such as food and clothes.

Then, just when you think these guys are never going to be able to apply this to their lives, He drops the gospel bomb.

> But seek first the kingdom of God and his righ-
> teousness, and all these things will be added to
> you. (Matt. 6:33)

A lot of people think of this as the biggest stressor of all. "Oh man, if I'm not seeking Jesus all the time, I'm done for!" I don't think that is the correct reading of this text. Jesus is saying, "Pursue Me, and I'll take care of the rest."

"Say yes to Me."

"Follow Me."

That's the biggest of all the *dos*. The rest take care of themselves.

Again and again, through the Gospels and epistles, we see this play out, but you have to go on a *do hunt*.

Let's give it a try with some familiar passages. Since we are already dealing with anxiety, let's start there.

> Do not be anxious about anything, but in everything by prayer and supplication with thanksgiving let your requests be made known to God. (Phil. 4:6)

If we focus on the *don't*, we can't hope to even obey this verse. *Don't be anxious!* Are you kidding me? Just reading that makes me anxious! It's even worse because it says, "Do not be anxious about anything."

But let's forget about the *don't* for a second and hunt for the *do*. "In everything by prayer and supplication with thanksgiving let your requests be made known to God." This verse is giving us the antidote for anxiety: prayer. Not just prayer, but thankful prayer. And not just thankful prayer, but thankful prayer to God. You see, this verse is reminding us of our position in Christ. Since we are seated with Him at the right hand of God the Father in the heavenly places, we have only to "look to the left" (metaphorically speaking) and pray to our dad. This is a very important verse for me right now because I am writing this less than five days from the deadline my publisher has given me to turn in this manuscript. Five days, and I still have a lot to write, more to edit, and a fair share of things to be anxious about.

But instead of freaking out about this looming deadline, I attempted the *do* and recruited some help. I asked my church to pray for me, and many of them have been texting and tweeting at me to let me know they are thankful I am writing this book and they are praying that God will help me use my time well.

Oddly, I slept like a baby last night, and I am just realizing why. God answered my (and my church's) prayers.

That's how you *do* the *do*.

Let's look at another verse.

> Let no one despise you for your youth, but set
> the believers an example in speech, in conduct, in
> love, in faith, in purity. (1 Tim. 4:12)

Let's be honest. "Older people" have a tendency to look down on "younger people." I used the quotation marks because I could be referring to a second grader looking down on a first grader or a guy with a gray beard looking down on a guy with a hipster beard.

It would be really easy (and very inappropriate) for a younger person to focus on the *don't* in this passage, declaring, "I am not going to let you look down on me!" But that would, quite literally, mean the younger person would be missing the point of the verse. It's the *do* that's important. "Set the believers an example in speech, in conduct, in love, in faith, in purity." If you *do* that, the *don't* takes care of itself.

Here's an example from Paul that looks like one big long *don't*. But go on a *do hunt* and see what you find:

"All things are lawful for me," but not all things are helpful. "All things are lawful for me," but I will not be dominated by anything. "Food is meant for the stomach and the stomach for food"—and God will destroy both one and the other. The body is not meant for sexual immorality, but for the Lord, and the Lord for the body. And God raised the Lord and will also raise us up by his power. Do you not know that your bodies are members of Christ? Shall I then take the members of Christ and make them members of a prostitute? Never! Or do you not know that he who is joined to a prostitute becomes one body with her? For, as it is written, "The two will become one flesh." But he who is joined to the Lord becomes one spirit with him. Flee from sexual immorality. Every other sin a person commits is outside the body, but the sexually immoral person sins against his own body. Or do you not know that your body is a temple of the Holy Spirit within you, whom you have from God? You are not your own, for you were bought with a price. So glorify God in your body. (1 Cor. 6:12–20)

See the *do*? It's in the last verse. "Glorify God in your body." Why? Paul's argument is right in the middle: "Do you not know that your bodies are members of Christ?" So many people who struggle with sexual immorality do so by focusing on the *don't*.

"I will not look at porn."

"I will not shack up with my girlfriend."

Try this one on for size: "Because I am part of Jesus's body, I will glorify God with it."

Do the *do*.

That's how you obey. Oh, and just in case you start feeling proud of yourself for getting this right, remember this verse:

> But he gives more grace. Therefore it says, "God opposes the proud, but gives grace to the humble." (James 4:6)

I used to focus on the second half of this verse (I even had it memorized).

"I will not be proud."

Then I saw the *do*: God "gives grace to the humble." And when I mess up, all I have to do is swing to the first part of the verse and remember that when I do, God "gives more grace."

We need all the grace we can get. Sometimes it seems like we fail more often than we succeed. I don't know about you, but sometimes my spiritual life seems like one step forward, a thousand steps back. It also seems like the older I get, the more sin I see in my life. I'm not sure if it's because I am sinning more (I sure hope not) or I am more acutely aware of my sin (which I really want to chalk up to maturity). One way or another, I am glad for every ounce of grace God wants to send my way.

DISCUSSION QUESTIONS

Coach Rob came crashing down on the ice when he least expected it. Then he was embarrassed and didn't want anyone to know. What can we learn from Coach Rob as we walk out onto the ice of obedience?

"Trying to obey God isn't the biggest danger. The real threat to our faith is when we actually succeed in obeying." How can it be a threat to our faith when we actually obey?

What is the purpose of our obedience to Jesus supposed to be? When we obey, what does this show the world?

Three common strategies to get people to obey are reward (if you do, you will get), duty (you will because you have to), and fear (you will or else). What are the strategies that have been used for you, whether in childhood or the workplace or significant relationships?

Do you use any of these strategies to get your own children, employees, or other people to comply? Do they work? Why is a reward, duty, or fear not the right way to motivate people to obey God? Do you think the church as a whole ever uses these? What are the effects of these particular motivators for Christians?

First John 3:6–10 is a tough passage to interpret. Do you agree with the author's interpretation? Why or why not?

A Christian's spiritual growth is typically a long and slow process. Why do you think people are surprised or frustrated when their own spiritual growth takes so long? Should they be? How do you feel about the process of your own spiritual growth?

"We are not in the completing business. God is." When you think about God being the one completing your spiritual growth instead of yourself, does this change anything?

How can people *know* they are saved?

What is the problem with trying to create our own "fruit"? Where does true fruit come from?

"I know, therefore, I obey; I obey, therefore, I know that I know." Which half of this equation do you wrestle with more? Do you struggle more with the "Now that I'm a Christian, I can do whatever I want" attitude (part 1) or the "Am I really a Christian" (part 2) doubt?

For those who struggle more with the first part of the equation: When Jesus comes back, He will evaluate how well we lived our lives on mission for Him. How would that evaluation go if He came back today? Do you value what He values? Are you leveraging all you have for His sake? Are you taking sin seriously?

For those who struggle more with the second part of the equation: The fruit (aka, obedience) in our lives is an indicator of our faith, but we can place unreasonable expectations on how much fruit we should be seeing in a certain amount of time. The apostle John tells us in 1 John 3:2 that "what we will be has not yet appeared; but we know that when he appears we shall be like him." When you stumble or mess up, how can you still be sure that you are saved? Consider the message in 1 John 3:2–3 and talk about how "it's never about what you do—it's always about what Jesus has done and what He will do."

As you try to live your life for God, do you tend to focus more on the "dos" or the "don'ts"?

Is there any particular area of your life where you are struggling to obey what the Bible says? Have you been focusing on the "dos" or the "don'ts" in your attempts? What does the Bible say to *do* in this particular area? What are some practical ways you could start implementing the "do"?

PART FOUR

SET FREE *TO*

For you were called to freedom, brothers. Only do not use
your freedom as an opportunity for the flesh, but through
love serve one another. For the whole law is fulfilled in
one word: "You shall love your neighbor as yourself."

Galatians 5:13–14

The Bible clearly says that God created everything for His own glory (Isa. 43:6–7; Eph. 1:4–6) and the fame of Jesus (Col. 1:15–20; Heb. 1:3). Since God is love, that glory finds its ultimate expression in love. With Adam's first sin (Rom. 5:12), love was trapped outside of the box while our pursuit of glory for ourselves kept us inside. Instead of love manifesting in the glory of God, humankind selfishly chased after those things that would lift us up. This sinful pursuit spun the world into chaos, hate, and indifference.

But God's sovereignty over all things meant love was going to win out. In the words of the Old Testament character Joseph, as said to his brothers who had sinned against him, "As for you, you meant evil against me, but God meant it for good, to bring it about that many people should be kept alive, as they are today" (Gen. 50:20).

Through the wilderness we created with our sin, God cut a pathway of love by sending Jesus to live a sinless life, die on the cross, rise again, and ascend to the right hand of the Father. This stunning act of love lifts all who believe out of the box to where Jesus is (Rom. 3:22). Now, as Jesus's followers, siblings, and friends, we glorify our Father by using our freedom to love.

CHAPTER 9

SET FREE *TO LOVE*

I love trying to figure out how things work. My mom claims this started at a very young age when I took apart the dining room table with a spoon. As I got older, I moved on to disassembling my bike, playing around in the guts of my computer, and, most recently, failing to restore a 1979 Fiat Spider convertible someone sold me for a dollar.

In the futile process of trying to get the car running, I learned about an amazing piece of technology that has been around for thousands of years: the flywheel. In layman's terms (the only ones I understand), a flywheel is a heavy disk that takes a whole lot of *oomph* to get going. The cool thing about the flywheel is once it is spinning at a fast enough pace, it takes just as much *oomph* to get it to stop. To keep it going, all you need is a gentle push at certain intervals.

Pottery wheels, sewing machines, toys, and even my 1979 Fiat Spider rely on flywheels to deliver consistent power. If you didn't have a flywheel in your car, it would leap in the air every time the pistons fired and make for a very rough ride.

THE FLYWHEEL OF LOVE

Our universe runs on a flywheel as well—the flywheel of love. One of the great theological concepts in the Bible is that God is not only the creator of all things but the sustainer of them as well (Col. 1:17; Heb. 1:3). He is the One who gave this giant world the big *oomph* it needed to get started, and He continues to nudge it along. Amazingly, God invites us into His work and allows our love to be part of the nudging.

WHAT IS LOVE?

We have to be really careful when we start talking about love because this is one of those places we have a tendency to take a worldly definition of something and try to squish it into the Bible. When we do that, we can mistakenly pervert what being a loving follower of Jesus is. Our cultural definitions of love often start too narrow, declaring that the person who is the receiver of love gets to define it and redefine it at will. If that is true, then it logically leads to a definition that is too broad because anything and everything will pass as love for *somebody*.

John Piper reminds us of the danger of that approach to love:

> Not *feeling* loved and not *being* loved are not the same. Jesus loved all people well. And many did not like the way he loved them....

> Emotional blackmail happens when a person
> equates his or her emotional pain with another
> person's failure to love. They aren't the same.[1]

Our world defines love in a decidedly unloving way when it declares that we must blindly accept who someone wants to be and how they want to live, no matter what. Let's be honest for a second. If Jesus had loved us that way, we would all be on our way to hell. My life is filled with attitudes and actions that contradict how God set up this world. It would have been fundamentally unloving for Jesus to let me stay there, separated from Him for all eternity.

Now does that mean we should become the caricature of a Christian "Bible thumper," yelling at all *those sinners* to repent? Certainly not. Instead, we need a definition of love, and whatever Dictionary.com has to offer us isn't going to cut it. We need to get our definition from God Himself. Paul, in his exhortation to the Philippian church, gives a helpful reminder of how that love plays out in the life of a follower of Jesus:

> And it is my prayer that your love may abound
> more and more, with knowledge and all discern-
> ment, so that you may approve what is excellent,
> and so be pure and blameless for the day of Christ,
> filled with the fruit of righteousness that comes
> through Jesus Christ, to the glory and praise of
> God. (Phil. 1:9–11)

Love that abounds is love that is overflowing with the fruit of the Spirit (love, joy, peace, patience, kindness, goodness, faithfulness, gentleness, and self-control), coupled with both knowledge and discernment. We consider what is truthful, and we wisely, carefully, and gently apply it. We "approve what is excellent," which simply means we agree with God on what His definition of excellent is. When all of this comes together, the fruit of righteousness will become even more evident in our lives to the glory and praise of God. But notice, as we have mentioned countless times already, where the fruit of righteousness comes from: Jesus Christ.

We can only truly live like this because we have been set free.

OKAY, SO WHAT IS LOVE, REALLY?

If we are to approve of what is excellent, and if love is the most excellent thing, it would be good for us to go to the source of love to define it for us: God.

The most famous passage of Scripture on love by far is 1 Corinthians 13. Tragically, most of us hear it read only at weddings. Now, it's not tragic to read it during a wedding ceremony—it most certainly applies there—but Paul was writing this to cantankerous Christians who were living decidedly in chains. The context of this letter isn't a sweet wedding with a cute flower girl and a clueless ring bearer. Rather, Paul, in the entire book of 1 Corinthians, was chewing out some Christians for living in some decidedly non-Christian ways. Chapter 13 was written in the context of a firm rebuke for how the church was using the gifts God had given them.

Take a minute to read through Paul's words. Imagine he is using a loving yet stern tone:

> If I speak in the tongues of men and of angels, but have not love, I am a noisy gong or a clanging cymbal. And if I have prophetic powers, and understand all mysteries and all knowledge, and if I have all faith, so as to remove mountains, but have not love, I am nothing. If I give away all I have, and if I deliver up my body to be burned, but have not love, I gain nothing.
>
> Love is patient and kind; love does not envy or boast; it is not arrogant or rude. It does not insist on its own way; it is not irritable or resentful; it does not rejoice at wrongdoing, but rejoices with the truth. Love bears all things, believes all things, hopes all things, endures all things.
>
> Love never ends. As for prophecies, they will pass away; as for tongues, they will cease; as for knowledge, it will pass away. For we know in part and we prophesy in part, but when the perfect comes, the partial will pass away. When I was a child, I spoke like a child, I thought like a child, I reasoned like a child. When I became a man, I gave up childish ways. For now we see in a mirror dimly, but then face to face. Now I know in part; then I shall know fully, even as I have been fully known.

> So now faith, hope, and love abide, these
> three; but the greatest of these is love. (1 Cor. 13)

It feels different when you think of Paul with a strong and instructive tone, doesn't it? He was very concerned because the Corinthians' way of living didn't represent Jesus well. He knew that he needed to reorient their affections toward their position with Jesus, so he reminded them about some of the attributes of God (who is love) and Jesus (who laid down His life in love). He wanted them (and us) to remember that if we are *unloving*, we are *unlike* God.

On the other hand, when we live loving lives, we tell the world around us that we have been set free. So let's take a stroll through these thirteen verses about love.

> If I speak in the tongues of men and of angels,
> but have not love, I am a noisy gong or a clang-
> ing cymbal. And if I have prophetic powers,
> and understand all mysteries and all knowledge,
> and if I have all faith, so as to remove moun-
> tains, but have not love, I am nothing. If I give
> away all I have, and if I deliver up my body to
> be burned, but have not love, I gain nothing.
> (1 Cor. 13:1–3)

Paul started out with the gift the Corinthians desired most: speaking in tongues. They loved it. When they spoke in tongues, it gave them glory and made them feel kind of special (see Paul's rebuke for this attitude in 1 Cor. 12; 14). So Paul, like a good pastor, went right after that idol in their lives, and he elevated it to the ridiculous. He said, "I don't care if you are fluent in every single human language and Angel as well, you've got this whole thing out of whack if you aren't loving." Not only does he tell them they would be out of whack, he told them they would be annoying.

When my children were little, my brother-in-law upped the ante in our relationship by buying them a drum kit. Not a little-kid, gonna-fall-apart-the-first-time-you-use-it kit, but a full-on drum kit. We put it in the basement in a futile attempt to isolate the chaos, but it was to no avail. When the kids would sit at the drums, they would do what any kid who had never had a drum lesson does: they would bang away as loudly as they could! It didn't matter where you went in the house, you couldn't escape. That's why, as soon as they began to show a decreasing interest in the blasted thing, I quietly put it into storage where it gloriously gathered dust until the day my neighbor mercifully asked to borrow it for his son. I didn't hesitate to say yes.

Paul said if (and it's kind of a crazy big "if") he could figure out how to speak not just human languages but also the language angels spoke as well, it would make him an apostolic angelic rock star. People would flood to him to hear him say the most mundane things in the tongues of angels. But Paul knew if he practiced this gift without love, he would become an annoying jerk. He'd be nothing more than a drum set with a crazy toddler in the seat.

What if he had infallible prophetic powers with direct revelation from God? Not only that, but what if he knew everything and understood anything you could possibly run by him? That's where he went next. He even said he would use that knowledge to figure out how to command mountains to do his bidding. What then? Without love—and you can almost hear him pause—"Without love I *am nothing.*"

But Paul didn't stop there. He went up to another unheard-of level! He said, "What if I gave away everything I own and even volunteer to be burned to death as a martyr … what then?" Without love, he knew he would gain nothing.

So, let this sink in.

Paul was saying, "If I can speak any and all languages this world has ever devised as well as the language of angels *and* I get marching orders directly from God Himself *and* I can boss around mountains *and* I can take care of the poor *and* I am burned at the stake, I would be an annoying, worthless zero—if I did all of that in an unloving way."

Why? Because without love, all of those things would serve only to give Paul glory. You see, the problem with the Corinthians, and with us as well, is that we think what we do gains us value, worth, and standing. We think God is more pleased with us if we sell everything we have and give it to the poor, die as a martyr, or have more faith or more knowledge. Paul says, "No!"

God just wants us to be more loving. That's it.

The other stuff is great, but it pales in comparison to love, because without love, we are not representing Jesus well.

Without love, we aren't really living free.

To make sure his readers really understand what he is getting at, Paul dives into what love is and what it isn't. In describing these things, he reminds us of what God is and what we have been set free to do. Let's start with what love isn't.

LOVE DOESN'T ENVY

A few years ago, one of my best friends bought an amazing house. Shortly after he and his family moved in, they invited us over to see the place and hang out. It was a gorgeous mid-century modern house with lots of huge windows and a ton of character. When we had completed the tour, I turned to my friend and said, "You would not own this house if I had seen it first."

I wasn't being sarcastic. I meant it. I wanted his house, and I wanted him not to have it so I could.

What a jerk. To clarify, I mean, *I* was the jerk.

I have since repented to him and have become very excited for his family to have such a great place to live, but I am still shocked at how quickly I jumped to envy.

Remember the box we talked about way back in chapter 2? Envy is very clearly an "inside the box" attitude, isn't it? It looks around at the stuff trapped in here with us and picks out the best for ourselves. It is fundamentally unloving and doesn't represent Jesus at all. He took what He had and gave it to us, no strings attached.

LOVE DOESN'T BOAST

We are a very braggadocios culture.

Yeah, you better believe I spelled that word right. I know it looks wrong, but I know how to spell. I am the king speller. My word processor didn't even have to correct me on that one. I'm the guy people hand their papers to when they want their spelling checked.

And I'm sure you get my point.

We love to brag in our culture, and social media has not only made it more pervasive, but it's made it an expected part of life as well. People can't take a jog around the block anymore without posting, "I ran 1.7 miles today! #scenesfromarun." They can't go on a date without snapping a picture of their #smokinghotwife. The fact that *humblebrag* has become a word shows us how far we have sunk into the pit of self-congratulations.

For me, the hardest part of putting together the proposal for this book was the part where I had to sell myself to the publisher. By the way, I had a great point I was going to make, but as I typed that, I realized it was a humblebrag. Ugh.

LOVE ISN'T ARROGANT

Okay, Paul, now you aren't even playing fair! Why did you have to follow up boasting with arrogance? This is idiocy! Insanity! Garbage! I'm not even going to play ball anymore—I'm skipping to the next one.

LOVE ISN'T RUDE

Oh, for crying out loud. I can't believe I was just rude to the apostle Paul (and the Holy Spirit too). It's just that this loving thing is *so hard* and being rude is *so easy.*

If you pay attention, it's not hard to miss how rude our culture has become. People rarely hold doors for anyone anymore unless they would feel awkward not doing so, drivers are more concerned about saving thirty seconds than the person in the car ahead of them, and students and parents alike are rude to teachers.

But love isn't rude.

LOVE DOESN'T INSIST ON ITS OWN WAY

Each of us thinks we are right because, otherwise, we would change our minds! The remarkable thing is that when we thought we were right in our own ways (Rom. 5:8), Jesus lovingly showed us the right way to love by laying down His life (John 15:13). If I could be so wrong about how I live my life, it's quite possible I am wrong about some other stuff; therefore, I don't have to insist anymore on my own way.

LOVE ISN'T IRRITABLE

It's a well-known sociological fact that morning people marry night owls. I don't know if it's the "opposites attract" thing, but I know very few couples who are able to get this one synced up.

There is no better way to illustrate irritability than to ask a night owl to talk with you at 6:30 a.m. or a morning person after 9:00 p.m. That conversation isn't love.

LOVE ISN'T RESENTFUL

The word *resentful* in Greek literally means "counts up wrong-doing." The NIV translation gets this one right when it translates 1 Corinthians 13:5 "[love] keeps no record of wrongs." Remember how God treats our sins now that we are "in Christ"?

> For I will be merciful toward their iniquities,
> and I will remember their sins no more.
> (Heb. 8:12)

When we refuse to keep a record of other people's sins, we tell them about a God who does the same for us.

LOVE DOESN'T REJOICE AT WRONGDOING

This one sounds so sinister! Who rejoices at wrongdoing?

I do.

I love it when I see someone "get what is coming to them." Sometimes it's as small as watching "fail" videos on Instagram or as big as watching others' lives unravel because they didn't listen to sound, godly advice (usually from me).

All of these things are sinful because they are all unlike God. And yet, in our sin, they serve as our default position. Now that we are set free, we can see that Jesus hasn't been any of these things to us and He offers us a new way to live. And when we live this way, we clear the air around us and our lives serve as a giant arrow pointed at Him.

Now we're getting to what Paul says love actually is. This is what we look like when we love.

LOVE IS PATIENT

I am fairly certain patience doesn't come naturally to anyone, but God has been infinitely patient with us. One of the most challenging verses in Scripture is in 2 Peter, which says:

> The Lord is not slow to fulfill his promise as some count slowness, but is patient toward you, not wishing that any should perish, but that all should reach repentance. (3:9)

I used to think this was talking about God being patient toward non-Christians, waiting for them to repent. Then one day it struck me; Peter is writing to Christians. That means the object of God's patience is me. And you. And all Christians everywhere. God is being patient, waiting for us to share the good news of Jesus with those who are perishing without him.

Think about how amazing that is! God could just give up on us and figure out some sort of "plan B," but He is patient with us to get around to telling people the most important thing they need to hear. We could use a dose of that patience ourselves.

A very ironic place impatience seems to rear its ugly head is when supposedly mature Christians look down on other believers who are not as far along as they are spiritually. Often the very patience God extends to us in our spiritual growth is missing in our expectations of others.

LOVE IS KIND

"Love is kind" doesn't mean being "nice." Kindness is a willingness to step out and take care of people when they need help. Being kind means rolling up our sleeves and getting into the messiness of relationships with people.

I'm not sure if you have noticed, but it can get pretty complicated to help people out—it takes our time, our money, and our energy.

LOVE REJOICES WITH THE TRUTH

Let's be honest as we think a bit about this one. Sometimes the truth makes us cringe; we usually like little white lies better. In certain parts of the Bible, we want to dodge the culturally insensitive content and language. And most of the time, we are happier if no one knows about the sin we are hiding. But love rejoices in the truth.

LOVE BEARS EVERYTHING

What does it mean to "bear everything"? Literally, in the Greek, this means to "cover over or hide the faults of others."

Wait a minute. What about rejoicing with truth?

Think about a love that we can take and use to cover over the faults and weaknesses of other people. A person has some annoying or nagging fault? Cover it. Someone has a personality quirk that gets on your nerves? Hide it from yourself.

Love changes everything.

LOVE BELIEVES ALL THINGS

This doesn't mean we are naive or gullible. It means we trust. Barring any evidence to the contrary, we believe in people. We aren't suspicious, always trying to find the ulterior motive with people.

LOVE HOPES IN ALL THINGS

This means we live in a state of positive expectation. In tough relationships, we hope for the positive.

LOVE ENDURES ALL THINGS

I once heard someone say that to endure all things means to stand up under piles and piles and piles of misery. You suck it up and gut it out.

> Love is patient and kind; love does not envy or
> boast; it is not arrogant or rude. It does not insist
> on its own way; it is not irritable or resentful; it
> does not rejoice at wrongdoing, but rejoices with
> the truth. Love bears all things, believes all things,
> hopes all things, endures all things. (1 Cor. 13:4–7)

Isn't that a world you would love to live in?

We all would!

Oh, to have people treat us like this.

This just seems impossible, doesn't it? How on earth are we supposed to do this? Maybe that's exactly the point. None of us can come close to achieving this standard of love, yet God (lovingly) transforms us more and more into the (loving) image of Jesus. And when we love in countercultural ways, people around us are drawn to Him.

Justin Holcomb, coauthor of *Rid of My Disgrace*, wrote this on his blog a few years ago:

> Love for God and others is the fruit of the miracle
> of regeneration and the Holy Spirit's work within
> us. The Holy Spirit begins empowering us to want
> to love, giving us the ability to love, and causing us
> to know the love of God.[2]

This is not a new law for us to follow. Love is the fruit of the Spirit—it's what God does in us, not what we try to muster in our own strength, as if we could pay God back.

As God produces love for Him and others in our hearts, we get to join Him in His mission of announcing reconciliation to the world. God works in our hearts to cause us to delight in what He delights in. "We love because he first loved us" (1 John 4:19). Because God has loved us so well in Christ, we are freed to love Him and love others.

It's not that we need to make ourselves more loving; we get to be more loving because of Jesus!

> Love never ends. As for prophecies, they will pass away; as for tongues, they will cease; as for knowledge, it will pass away. (1 Cor. 13:8)

The Corinthians loved the big showy gifts that gave them the glory. Prophecy and tongues were at the top of their list. But Paul said, "Guys, those gifts are going away. Even knowledge has a shelf life."

But not love.

Love is not going away because God is love and *He* is not going away.

> For we know in part and we prophesy in part, but when the perfect comes, the partial will pass away. (1 Cor. 13:9–10)

Whatever we think we know is incomplete. As I have written this book, I have learned a lot of stuff, and I can't wait for the negative reviews to come out so I can learn some more. One day, the perfect will come. What does that mean? On that day, all that is imperfect will be gone. Everything in the box will disappear. But those with Christ will still be. We'll have no more sin, no more sorrow—we'll be totally free forever!

> When I was a child, I spoke like a child, I thought like a child, I reasoned like a child. When I became a man, I gave up childish ways. (1 Cor. 13:11)

It's funny to me when adults talk to and try to negotiate with their children as if they were just little adults. They aren't. They're kids, and they think, reason, and speak like they are! And how does a child speak? Simplistic, selfish, narrow, unreasonable, illogical. That's how you speak when you are a slave to sin. But one day …

> For now we see in a mirror dimly, but then face to face. Now I know in part; then I shall know fully, even as I have been fully known. (1 Cor. 13:12)

One day, you will be fully known. Deep down, we want this. And deep down, we don't. It terrifies us. We think, *If God really knew who I really am, He wouldn't love me.* But He does.

He loves you so much He sent Jesus to set you free from the Law, religion, sin, guilt, and shame. He set you free to love by giving the flywheel of love the big *oomph* it needed to get started.

KEEPING THE FLYWHEEL SPINNING

John, who liked to call himself "the disciple Jesus loved" (see John 13:23), didn't write about only obedience in 1 John (as we saw in the previous chapter); he also showed clearly how obedience is intrinsically tied to, you guessed it, love.

> Whoever says he is in the light and hates his brother is still in darkness. Whoever loves his brother abides in the light, and in him there is no cause for stumbling. (1 John 2:9–10)

> By this we know love, that [Jesus] laid down his life for us, and we ought to lay down our lives for the brothers. (1 John 3:16)

> Beloved, let us love one another, for love is from God, and whoever loves has been born of God and knows God. Anyone who does not love does not know God, because God is love. In this the love of God was made manifest among us, that God sent his only Son into the world, so that we might live through him. In this is love, not that we have loved God but that he loved us and sent his Son to be the propitiation for our sins. Beloved, if God so loved us, we also ought to love one another. No one has ever seen God; if we

love one another, God abides in us and his love is
perfected in us. (1 John 4:7–12)

When we pull all of this together, we can see John's argument
is clear:

- God is love (1 John 4:8).
- God loved us by sending Jesus (1 John 4:9).
- We should follow God's example and love one
  another (1 John 3:16; 4:11).
- When we abide in Jesus, we will love (1 John
  2:9–10; 4:7, 12).
- When we love, God abides in us and His love is
  perfected in us (1 John 4:12).

Love is what we are set free to do! In the previous chapter, we
talked about how we are set free to obey, and now we see that obedience ultimately manifests itself in love. This means we can take
the same equation we used in the previous chapter and substitute
the word *love* for the word *obey*. I know, therefore, I love; I love,
therefore, I know that I know.

When we love, we give this cosmic flywheel a tiny push and
tell the world that we know Jesus. It's not even that God needs
us to help Him keep the thing going—He's got that covered.
Nevertheless, He has invited us to play a small part in His sov-
ereign plan in the same way I used to invite my kids to take part
in some project I was working on around the house. One of the

big ways He includes us in His plan is through the *one anothers* in Scripture.

ONE ANOTHERING

The New Testament uses the phrase "one another" 101 times. A close inspection shows that 33 of the *one anothers* are narrative descriptions such as "they said to one another," "they argued with one another," or "they trampled one another" (seriously—check out Luke 12:1). Once we have eliminated those, we are left with a solid 68 *one anothers* with an overwhelmingly consistent theme: love.

In fact, the most common *one another* is "love one another," which appears 18 times, followed by "greet one another with a holy kiss" (not kidding) with 4 instances and "be at peace, or live in harmony, with one another" and "encourage one another" racking up 3 instances apiece. If you're doing the math at home, you know that leaves us with 40 random *one anothers*.

Each and every one of them is really just another fancy way of saying "love one another." Check out these lists:

DO:

- love one another (John 13:34 twice; John 13:35; John 15:12; John 15:17; Rom. 12:10; Gal. 5:13; 1 Thess. 3:12; 4:9; 2 Thess. 1:3; 1 Pet. 1:22; 4:8; 1 John 3:11, 23; 4:7, 11–12; 2 John v. 5)

- greet one another with a holy kiss (Rom. 16:16; 1 Cor. 16:20; 2 Cor. 13:12; 1 Pet. 5:14)
- be at peace, or live in harmony, with one another (Mark 9:50; Rom. 12:16; Rom. 15:5)
- encourage one another (1 Thess. 4:18; 5:11; Heb. 10:25)
- wash one another's feet (John 13:14)
- instruct, or exhort, one another (Rom. 15:14; Heb. 3:13)
- do not deprive one another of sex (very import-ant but only for married people!) (1 Cor. 7:5)
- wait for one another (1 Cor. 11:33)
- care for one another (1 Cor. 12:25)
- comfort one another (2 Cor. 13:11)
- agree with one another (2 Cor. 13:11)
- serve one another (Gal. 5:13; 1 Pet. 4:10)
- bear one another's burdens (Gal. 6:2)
- bear with one another (Eph. 4:2; Col. 3:13)
- be kind to one another (Eph. 4:32)
- forgive one another (Eph. 4:32; Col. 3:13)
- sing to one another (Eph. 5:19; Col. 3:16)
- submit to one another (Eph. 5:21)
- build up one another (1 Thess. 5:11)
- do good to one another (1 Thess. 5:15)
- stir one another up to love and good works (Heb. 10:24)
- confess your sins to one another (James 5:16)

- show hospitality to one another (1 Pet. 4:9)
- show humility toward one another (1 Pet. 5:5)
- have fellowship with one another (1 John 1:7)

DON'T:

- compare yourself with one another (2 Cor. 10:12 twice)
- bite and devour one another (Gal. 5:15 twice)
- provoke one another (Gal. 5:26)
- envy one another (Gal. 5:26)
- lie to one another (Col. 3:9)
- hate one another (Titus 3:3)
- speak evil of one another (James 4:11)
- grumble against one another (James 5:9)

Can you imagine a world like this where envy, hate, and lies take a backseat to forgiveness, kindness, and hospitality? Can you dream of a place where everyone actively looks out for one another and thinks more about how to *serve them* rather than *being served by them*? That world isn't a far-fetched dream—it's what living as an unchained follower of Jesus is really like! We represent a king who has set us free. Paul went so far as to say:

> [God] gave us the ministry of reconciliation; that is, in Christ God was reconciling the world to himself, not counting their trespasses against

> them, and entrusting to us the message of rec-
> onciliation. Therefore, we are ambassadors for
> Christ, God making his appeal through us. We
> implore you on behalf of Christ, be reconciled to
> God. (2 Cor. 5:18–20)

We are in the reconciling business. That's why the *one anothers* are so important! When we live together in a community like this, people will want to know why our lives look so different.

Recently, I heard the story of a guy in our church who unexpectedly lost his job. When his small group gathered for their weekly meeting, he asked them to pray for his situation. They did, and then they *one anothered* him like crazy. Over the span of the next week, they filled his pantry with groceries ("care for one another"), paid his mortgage and utilities ("do good to one another"), helped him put a new résumé together ("serve one another"), and called to check up on his wife and kids ("encourage one another"). Talk about "stirring one another up to love and good works"!

Then there's the single mom and her kids who lost their home to a fire. People in our church let her live in their basement until she found a new place ("show hospitality to one another").

At the time of this writing, one of my copastors' sons is battling cancer, and he and his family have seen people line up to obey the loving command to "bear one another's burdens" with everything from providing gas cards to cooking meals when they have a chance to come home from the hospital for a few days.

This sort of thing causes people to ask, "Why?"

"Why are you paying that guy's mortgage?"

"Why are you letting those people live with you?"

"Why are you paying for gas for that family's car?"

In these moments, it becomes clear what Jesus was talking about when He said, "By this all people will know that you are my disciples, if you have love for one another" (John 13:35).

Love is what Christianity in action looks like; it's what we are set free to do!

DISCUSSION QUESTIONS

How do you define love? Discuss the world's definition versus God's definition.

Read 1 Corinthians 13, but as you read through it, imagine it being said in a firm, stern rebuke rather than joyously at an emotional wedding ceremony. Does this change the way you see what Paul is saying?

If we are unloving, we are unlike God. On the other hand, when we live loving lives, we tell the world around us that we have been set free. Talk about the Christians who have influenced your life, whether for good or for bad. What have their lives told you about God?

What does it actually look like for us to "live loving lives"? Give some practical examples.

Anything and everything we do for God, if it's done *without love*, is worthless. Do you ever think certain things you do give you more value, worth, or standing with God? What are some of these things? Does doing them represent Jesus well?

Love is *not*: envious, boastful, arrogant, rude, insistent on its own way, irritable, resentful, or joyful with wrongdoing. Love *is*: patient, kind, rejoicing with the truth, bearing everything, believing all things, hoping in all things, and enduring all things. Are these things what come to mind when we think of love in our everyday lives? Is there anything on this list that surprises you or that might be contrary to our culture's definition of love?

The patience God extends to us as He waits for us to mature spiritually is staggering. Why do you think Christians often have higher expectations than even God does for spiritual growth, both for ourselves and in others?

Being kind is different from being nice. Talk about the difference, and then discuss some examples of true kindness.

Sometimes hard truth can feel unloving. Yet true love "rejoices with the truth." What are some of the culturally insensitive parts

SET FREE *TO LOVE*

of the Bible that we might rather stay quiet about? Is it more loving if we address these issues or stay quiet about them?

What does "love bears everything" mean? What are some examples of what this looks like?

Love believes, hopes, and endures all things. This means we trust people, giving them the benefit of the doubt and hoping for positive transformation. Is this how we commonly interact with others? Is this how people typically treat you? Is it how you treat others?

When we love others, it's a way for us to play a small part in God's big plan that He's invited us into. He doesn't need us, but He lets us participate anyway. Why do you think God invites us into this? Do you think of loving others as your way to take part in God's plan?

"Can you dream of a place where everyone actively looks out for one another and thinks more about how to *serve them* rather than *being served by them*? That world isn't a far-fetched dream—it's what living as an unchained follower of Jesus is really like!" Do you feel like this describes the community you are a part of?

Is love the defining factor of the Christianity you've experienced? Describe what Christianity in action has looked like for you.

CHAPTER 10

SET FREE *TO LIVE FREE*

North Korea.

Just hearing those words breaks my heart.

Imagine what it must be like to live in a country with such a notoriously repressive regime, being constantly bombarded with mythical stories about the awful world outside your borders. This steady diet of propaganda is a masterful distraction from your physical diet that keeps you on the brink of starvation.

A few years ago, I stumbled onto an interview with Shin Dong-hyuk, a man who was born in a prison known only as Camp 14. His father and mother were born in the same prison because his uncles had defected to South Korea. North Korea has a well-known policy of "three generations of punishment" they inflict on those who oppose (or are even suspected of opposing) the government. Because Shin was born in the prison, he knew no other life. In his mind, the entire world was Camp 14, and there were only two types of people in the world: prisoners and guards. You were born as one or the other, and you lived your entire life that way. When asked by Anderson Cooper if he ever thought about escaping, he replied, "No. Never. What I thought was that the society outside the camp would be similar to that inside the camp."[1]

Every day, Shin did the same thing: he obeyed. He was told what to do and he did it. He was told to eat a small portion of corn gruel and cabbage for every meal, and he just assumed that was how it had to be. He was a prisoner. For twenty-three years, he was always hungry and tired from daily hard labor.

But Shin said everything changed in one day. A new prisoner named Park was brought to Camp 14, and with him came tales of a different world on the other side of the electrified fence. He talked about living in cities and traveling to China. But one particular thing Park talked about defined freedom in Shin Dong-hyuk's mind more than anything else: broiled chicken. Park told him that outside the electrified fence of his world was another world where you could eat broiled chicken—and you could eat it *anytime you wanted.*

Shin had never eaten chicken. But he knew what chicken tasted like: freedom.

This quest for broiled chicken led Shin and Park to attempt to escape over the electrified fence. Park touched the fence first and immediately died. An untold number of volts coursed through his body and stopped his heart. His body became a bridge over which Shin was able to climb to freedom. That day he became the only person to ever escape from Camp 14 and live to tell the tale.

Shin Dong-hyuk is no longer a prisoner. He now lives in South Korea and eats broiled chicken whenever he wants. This chicken, along with his freedom, was purchased by a friend who gave his life for him.

As we come to the last chapter of this book, you may feel like Shin, and you should—because part of his story is our own. Each one of us was born as a prisoner in chains; it's the only life we knew. Our prison guard (sin) told us to do something, and we obeyed. But then one day, a guy named Jesus showed up with stories of a different way of living in a world we'd never even dreamed about. Although escape seemed impossible, a bridge was built for us. He laid down His life for us so we would be able to climb over Him to freedom. There is no way we could ever make it over that electrified fence alone—it's only when we believe that what Jesus says about the outside world is true and we take that step of faith onto His back that we can get there. It is by grace alone, through faith alone, that we are set free.

In the book of Galatians, Paul declares, "I do not nullify the grace of God, for if righteousness were through the law, then Christ died for no purpose" (2:21).

Imagine for a moment what would have happened if Shin Dong-hyuk had escaped from Camp 14 but shortly thereafter decided he didn't like the outside world and eating chicken anytime he wanted. What if he had decided hard labor was a better idea and turned himself back in to the prison?

Even the thought is ludicrous—if for no other reason than that his friend's death would have been for no purpose.

What if, after he had spent some time in the outside world, someone came to Shin and said, "I know you are enjoying your freedom, but you really belong in a different camp." I suspect he would fight to his dying breath to stay out of that camp.

But that was exactly what was happening in Galatia.

Christians who had been set free by Jesus were being told to put their chains back on, to reinstitute the Law that Jesus had fulfilled and build a Gentile version of the Jewish religion.

And the crazy thing? They were going along with it.

That's why Paul started chapter 3 with the words "O foolish Galatians!" (Gal. 3:1).

Let me retranslate that for you: "You *idiots*!" The very point of Christianity is that you have been set free! When you try to place chains back on yourself, you are making a mockery of Jesus's sacrifice. So Paul said:

> O foolish Galatians! Who has bewitched you? It was before your eyes that Jesus Christ was publicly portrayed as crucified. (Gal. 3:1)

Just a few years before, when Paul had helped plant the church in Galatia, he had clearly shared the gospel of Jesus with them. The words "publicly portrayed" were like a sponsored Facebook post plastered on thousands of walls. And yet these other guys had jumped onto the site and launched into a comment campaign undercutting the gospel message. To counteract these men, Paul asked the Galatians five rhetorical questions, which are great final thoughts for us.

> Let me ask you only this: Did you receive the
> Spirit by works of the law or by hearing with
> faith? (Gal. 3:2)

Question 1: Why did the Spirit come to live in you?

    (A) You were such a great person and so obedient to the Law

    (B) Because you placed your faith in Jesus

The answer? (B). If you said (A), go back to chapter 1.

The Galatians weren't even Jewish, so they never thought about keeping the Law until someone came along and told them they had to. Like Shin Dong-hyuk, they started out their lives trapped in sin, not knowing any better. It was only *after* Jesus set them free (by faith) that they encountered some guys who told them to start obeying the Law.

> Are you so foolish? (Gal. 3:3)

Question 2: Are you idiots?

    (A) Yes

    (B) No

The answer? Hopefully (B), but probably (A). If you don't answer (A) at least part of the time, you're fooling yourself.

Having begun by the Spirit, are you now being
perfected by the flesh? (Gal. 3:3)

Here's the logic Paul is laying out. If you cannot set yourself
free, what makes you think you can make yourself more free once
you become a Christian? Hence, his question.

Question 3: Which of the following matures you as a believer?
  (A) Your own effort
  (B) The Holy Spirit

I appreciate the reminder from Steve Brown that every
Christian is given two gifts from God, a picture and a mirror.
He explains:

> You're supposed to look into the mirror and
> contemplate the picture. The mirror shows
> you what you look like now and the picture,
> well, that's a picture of Jesus. God says, "That
> is what you are and this is what you will
> become." Sometimes it'll hurt and sometimes
> you'll mess it up; sometimes you won't believe
> it's happening. But trust me on this, one day
> you'll look just like Jesus. So look in the mirror
> and wince but don't forget to look at the pic-
> ture and rejoice. Rejoice and relax too. God has
> promised to get the job done.[2]

When we become Christian, the Holy Spirit starts the pains-taking work of restoring us to looking more and more like Jesus. It's not our work to do.

The answer? Well, after such a long hint, I'd be very surprised if you guessed any answer but (B).

> Did you suffer so many things in vain—if indeed
> it was in vain? (Gal. 3:4)

This is an interesting question, very specifically tailored to the young Galatian church. Paul had warned them, back in Acts 14, that they were going to face trials because of their faith in Jesus. Some of them would lose their jobs, their families, even their lives. This is so foreign to us! I was talking to someone recently who told me about Chinese Christians who are evangelizing in the Middle East. They know they may die or lose everything, but that's how they live in the underground church already. They know it is worth it because they know it's the truth.

Paul was basically asking the Galatians …

Question 4: Did you suffer for a lie?

(A) Yes

(B) No

If they lost jobs and families and lives to preach the gospel of Jesus and then it turned out that they really only had to be good people (and they could do that on their own), was it really worth it? Was it all a lie?

The answer? (B). When we suffer, we suffer for the truth, not for a lie.

And now Paul's final question (and this one is masterful):

> Does he who supplies the Spirit to you and works miracles among you do so by works of the law, or by hearing with faith—just as Abraham "believed God, and it was counted to him as righteousness"? (Gal. 3:5–6)

One of the ways that God made His message known in the early church was through signs and wonders, miraculous events that had no explanation other than coming from God. The dead were raised and people born blind were healed and could see! Paul was essentially asking …

Question 5: On what basis does God perform miracles?

(A) Because He notices you are so awesome and it makes Him want to

(B) Because you have heard the gospel and placed your faith in Him

The answer? (B). See question 1.

When you boil it down, these five questions are really only one question and there really is only one answer.

The big (and only) question: Who saves?
The big (and only) answer: God does, through Jesus.

Paul used the example of Abraham, who "believed God, and it was counted to him as righteousness."

Who was Abraham? He was the father of the Jews. In Galatia, some people were saying that all the new believers needed to become Jews in order to be Christian, and to prove it, they should follow the Mosaic Law (that Moses brought the people) and be circumcised (which was something God started with Abraham). So Paul brought them right back to Abraham and quoted Genesis:

> And [God] brought [Abraham] outside and said, "Look toward heaven, and number the stars, if you are able to number them." Then he said to him, "So shall your offspring be." And he believed the LORD, and he counted it to him as righteousness. (Gen. 15:5–6)

Abraham believed in God when He said his offspring would be as hard to count as the stars in the sky, and because of his belief, God said to him, "You are righteous." Then, two chapters later, Abraham was circumcised. Therefore, Paul was saying that Abraham and all the people of God in the Old Testament were saved by faith just as we are today. They were saved because they looked forward to God fulfilling His promise. We are saved because we look back and see that, through Jesus, God has fulfilled His promise.

> Know then that it is those of faith who are the sons of Abraham. And the Scripture, foreseeing that God would justify the Gentiles by faith, preached the gospel beforehand to Abraham, saying, "In you shall all the nations be blessed." So then, those who are of faith are blessed along with Abraham, the man of faith. (Gal. 3:7–9)

Paul was essentially saying, "You guys think you need to become Jews to become Christians? Don't worry about it! If you have placed your faith in Jesus, you are sons of Abraham."

If you grew up in the church, it's likely you can sing this song with me: "Father Abraham had many sons …"

Even though many of us are not Jewish, we sing this song because we are sons and daughters of Abraham. We are part of his family of faith. All the nations of the world will be blessed through Jesus, who came from the line of Abraham. And because of Jesus, we are set free.

Every time Shin Dong-hyuk eats a piece of broiled chicken, not only does he remember the freedoms he has, but his mind goes to the children being born in Camp 14 now. He wants them to taste the freedom he tastes, so he has dedicated his life to communicating the human rights atrocities of North Korea.

That's what we do with the freedoms we have.

We celebrate our freedom and do everything we can to tell other people that they, too, can be set free because they have a friend who laid down His life for them.

Remember Kate, the woman from my small group in chapter 1 who just couldn't believe God was pleased with her? For several weeks, we reminded her emphatically that, because she was in Christ, God was pleased with her. She was no longer positionally chained up in the box. There were no conditions, no *ifs*, *ands*, or *buts*.

God was pleased with her, period.

She could live free because she was free!

Kate decided she needed a daily reminder, so she wrote the words "God is pleased with you!" on a piece of paper and taped it to the mirror in her bathroom. Each morning as she rose to brush her teeth, she would read the words and shake her head in disbelief.

Until one day when it sank in.

Before she even walked into the bathroom, she was smiling.

She read the words aloud, and her smile grew. In that moment, she understood (and she would use the word *experienced*) the depth of the gospel in such a profound way that she couldn't have stopped smiling even if she had wanted to. That week when our small group met, she told us this story with excitement and then asked, "What do I do now?"

Before anyone could say anything, the wisest person in the room (my wife) quickly spoke up and declared, "Nothing. Now you do nothing."

Sometimes the best way to live free is to do nothing.

———————

DISCUSSION QUESTIONS

For prisoner Shin Dong-hyuk, Camp 14 was all that existed. It took a prisoner, Park, from outside the walls to come in and tell him about a world beyond what Shin knew, and that changed everything. Talk about how Park's life is a picture of what Jesus did for us.

Once Shin had escaped from Camp 14 and tasted freedom, there was no going back. Like Shin, we are no longer prisoners—we are out of the camp; we are *free*. And yet, like the Galatians, we often believe we aren't. We put on self-made chains that prohibit us from living the life God intends us to live. Are you living with any chains, whether self-made or put on by others?

Shin has dedicated his life to helping others know about what's going on in North Korea and trying to save others from the situation he himself was in. How can we use our freedom in order to save others who haven't yet met Jesus?

Do you believe God is pleased with you, *no matter what*? If not, what are some things you might do to help convince yourself and fully believe this is true?

"Sometimes the best way to live free is to do nothing." How do you interpret that sentence? Discuss what it means to live free.

As you come to the end of this book, what are some of the things that stood out to you? Thinking all the way back to the first chapter, is there anything you learned or considered that you hadn't before?

How has reading this book changed your thinking? How might it change how you live out your freedom in Christ?

TO MY NON-CHRISTIAN FRIENDS

Hey.

How's it going? I hope all is well.

I know the title of this afterword probably bugged you a little bit because it describes you as *non*-something and that seems a bit negative. I'm sorry about that. I couldn't figure out what to title this section, and this is the best I could do. I thought about "To My Spiritually Interested Friends" or something like that, but some of you, well, aren't. So I used the all-encompassing "non-Christian." No offense intended.

I gave you a copy of this book because I was thinking about you a lot when I was writing it.

My primary audience, which you know if you are reading this part last, is people who are Christians but don't feel their faith has made any real difference in how their lives "feel." You know I'm not a touchy-feely guy, but I run into people like this all the time. They started coming to church so they could sort out their spiritual interest. Perhaps they were feeling trapped by something—or life was going down the tubes and they needed some help. After becoming Christians and hanging around for a while, the shiny newness of it all faded away and they were left with … bleh. Worse, some of them felt even more trapped than they did before.

This whole thing gnaws at me because I know the freedom Jesus offers.

Hopefully, through our friendship, you have seen me live as a free person. I don't claim to have it all figured out (I am a recovering hypocrite, after all), but I have tried to represent Jesus the best I can to you.

That gets to the point of this letter. I secretly wrote this book for you.

I wanted you to see a picture of what it means to be a Christian, and I figured if I gave you a free book (and one that I wrote for that matter), maybe you would give it a read. I love you (in the least creepy way possible), and I would be devastated if you went through your whole life and no one told you that you were unknowingly enslaved. I became a pastor not because I didn't have any other options but because I wanted as many people as possible to hear about Jesus.

That includes you.

Especially you.

So, here's the bottom line: if you want to sit down and have a beer sometime to talk about this stuff, I would love to do it. And if this book sells well, I may even be willing to pay for the first round.

Your friend,
Noel

NEW TESTAMENT SURVEY ON THE LAW

Back in chapter 3, I promised you a biblical survey of the Law. The following research came from a sermon on the Law I gave a couple of years ago. I spent some time with my former assistant (Ryan Freitas) categorizing every single verse in the New Testament that references the Law. The results were incredibly eye opening, especially if you sit down and read them straight through in one sitting.

SUMMARY OF THE LAW

- "Whatever you wish that others would do to you, do also to them, for this is the Law and the Prophets" (Matt. 7:12).
- Love is the fulfillment of the Law (Rom. 13:10; Gal. 5:14; James 2:8).

- The greatest commandment in the Law is to love God and love others (Matt. 22:36–40; Luke 10:26–28).

PURPOSE OF THE LAW

- The Law judges and justifies (Rom. 2:12–13).
- When the Law is spoken to those under it, their mouths are stopped and the world is judged (Rom. 3:19).
- The Law brings knowledge of sin and counts it up (Rom. 3:20; 5:13; 7:8–9).
- The Law brings wrath (Rom. 4:15).
- The Law arouses sinful passions (Rom. 7:5) and increases trespasses (Rom. 5:20; Heb. 7:28).
- The Law is binding only when a person is alive (Rom. 7:1).
- The Law is holy, righteous, and good (Rom. 7:12, 16; 1 Tim. 1:8).
- The Law is good *if* used lawfully (1 Tim. 1:8–9).
- The Law is spiritual (Rom. 7:14).
- The Law is unable to save or give life (Rom. 8:3; Gal. 2:16; 3:21).
- The Law belongs to the Israelites (Rom. 9:4).
- The Law is the power of sin (1 Cor. 15:56).
- Those under the Law must obey *all* of the Law (Gal. 3:10, 12; 5:3; James 2:10).

- The Law was added because of transgressions (Gal. 3:19).
- The Law holds captive until faith comes (Gal. 3:23).
- The Law was a guardian until Jesus came (Gal. 3:24).
- The Law is not for the just, but for the lawless (1 Tim. 1:8–11).
- The Law made nothing perfect and cannot make anything perfect (Heb. 7:19; 10:1).
- The Law is only a shadow of the good to come (Heb. 10:1).

THE PURPOSE OF THE LAW IN JESUS

- Jesus did not abolish the Law, but He fulfilled it (Matt. 5:17).
- Not a dot of the Law will pass until all is accomplished (Matt. 5:18; Luke 16:16–17).
- The Law is about Jesus (Luke 24:44; John 1:45; 12:34; 15:25; Acts 28:23; Rom. 3:21).
- Jesus fulfilled the righteous requirement of the Law (Rom. 8:4).
- Jesus is the end of the Law for righteousness to everyone who believes (Rom. 10:4).
- Christ redeemed us from curse of the Law (Gal. 3:13).

- The Law was not overthrown but rather was upheld by faith (Rom. 3:31).
- Christ abolished the Law of commandments expressed in ordinances (Eph. 2:15).

FREEDOM AND THE LAW

- The Law does not bring freedom—belief in Jesus brings freedom (Acts 13:39).
- Paul was accused of teaching against the Law because he taught freedom from circumcision and customs (Acts 21:21).
- The righteousness of God has now been manifested apart from the Law (Rom. 3:21).
- Justification is not earned by works of the Law but by faith (Rom. 3:28; Gal. 2:16; 3:11).
- Sin will not have dominion because we are under grace and not under the Law (Rom. 6:14).
- You have died to the Law and been released from it (Rom. 7:4, 6; Gal. 2:19; 1 Cor. 9:20).
- The law of the Spirit of life has set you free in Christ Jesus from the Law of sin and death (Rom. 8:2).
- The righteous requirement of the Law is fulfilled in those who walk in the Spirit, not flesh (Rom. 8:4).

THE NEW LAW

- The new law is called the law of faith (Rom. 3:27; 4:16; Gal. 3:11).
- Released from the Law, we serve in a new way of the Spirit (Rom. 7:6).
- The law of the Spirit of life sets us free from the old Law (Rom. 8:2).
- The new law is called the law of Christ (1 Cor. 9:21).
- If we are led by the Spirit, we are not under the Law (Gal. 5:18).
- Bearing one another's burdens fulfills the law of Christ (Gal. 6:2).
- A change in the priesthood necessitates a change in the Law (Heb. 7:12).
- The new law is called the law of liberty (James 1:25).
- We should speak and act as if we are to be judged under the law of liberty (James 2:12).

MISCELLANEOUS VERSES ON THE LAW

- All of the Law is important, but some parts of it are weightier than others (Matt. 23:23).
- Paul was accused of teaching against Law (Acts 18:13; 21:28).

- Paul professed belief in the Law (Acts 24:14).
- Paul was not against the Law (Acts 25:8).
- The Law is written on all human hearts (Rom. 2:14–15).
- Those who boast in the Law dishonor God by breaking it (Rom. 2:17–23).
- The promise to Abraham did not come through the Law but through faith (Rom. 4:13).
- If the Law could save, faith would be null, the promise of God would be void, and Christ died for no purpose (Rom. 4:14; Gal. 2:21; Heb. 7:11).
- When the Law increases trespass, sin increases, and grace abounds; but this does not give a license to sin (Rom. 5:20; 6:15; Heb. 10:26–28).
- The Law is not sin (Rom. 7:7).
- Paul delighted in the Law, but he knew that the Law of sin waged war inside his body (Rom. 7:22–25).
- A fleshly mind does not and cannot submit to Law (Rom. 8:7).
- All things are lawful for a follower of Jesus, but not necessarily helpful; no one should be dominated by anything that doesn't build up (1 Cor. 6:12; 10:23).

- You are cursed if you rely on works of the Law (Gal. 3:10).
- The Law is not of faith (Gal. 3:12).
- Inheritance does not come by the Law (Gal. 3:18).
- The Law is not contrary to promise (Gal. 3:21).
- "Tell me, you who desire to be under the law, do you not listen to the law?" (Gal. 4:21).
- If you seek to be justified by the Law, you have fallen from grace (Gal. 5:4).
- Avoid quarrels about the Law (Titus 3:9).

NOTES

CHAPTER 1: FREEDOM SURE DOESN'T FEEL VERY FREE

1. Bruce A. Ware, *Father, Son, and Holy Spirit: Relationships, Roles, and Relevance* (Wheaton, IL: Crossway Books, 2005), 75.

CHAPTER 2: REALLY FREE BUT NOT REALLY FREE

1. For years, I searched for a simple, memorable definition of sin I could teach my congregation and repeat often in my preaching. My favorite came from Wayne Grudem, who defined sin as "any failure to conform to the moral law of God in act, attitude, or nature." I adapted his definition, using "failure to reflect the image of God," because I felt it made it more vivid and easier to remember. Wayne Grudem, *Bible Doctrine: Essential Teachings of the Christian Faith* (Grand Rapids, MI: Zondervan, 2014), 210.

2. At the time I wrote this paragraph, the Cubs were making quite a run and the play-offs were a very real possibility. If they won everything, you can call me a prophet. If they didn't, I'm sorry I jinxed it. It was totally my fault.

3. J. D. Greear, *Gospel* (Nashville: B&H, 2011), 48.

PART TWO: SET FREE *FROM*

1. "Colour Is in the Eye of the Beholder," BBC Horizon, BoreMe, accessed July 25, 2016, www.boreme.com/posting.php?id=30670#.Vq9wd8cvcRl.

CHAPTER 3: SET FREE *FROM THE LAW*

1. Stanley N. Gundry, ed., et al., *Five Views on Law and Gospel* (Grand Rapids, MI: Zondervan, 1999).

2. William McDavid, Ethan Richardson, and David Zahl, *Law and Gospel: A Theology for Sinners (and Saints)* (Charlottesville, VA: Mockingbird Ministries, 2015).

3. "Are Christians Expected to Obey the Old Testament Law?," Compelling Truth, accessed July 26, 2016, www.compellingtruth.org/Christian-OT -law.html#ixzz38ytIchK7.

CHAPTER 4: SET FREE *FROM RELIGION*

1. Quoted in "Christianity Is a Relationship Not a Religion," Dictionary of Christianese, accessed July 26, 2016, www.dictionaryofchristianese.com /christianity-is-a-relationship-not-a-religion/.

CHAPTER 5: SET FREE *FROM SIN*

1. Terry Virgo, *PlantMidwest Quarterly*, Restore Church, Detroit, May 12, 2015.

2. Aristotle, *Nicomachean Ethics*.

3. Ricky Van Veen, "You Are What You Tweet," TEDˣ, March 7, 2013, http://tedxtalks.ted.com/video/You-Are-What-You-Tweet-Ricky-Va.

4. Frank Zappa, "You Are What You Is," *You Are What You Is* © 1981 Barking Pumpkin.

5. Bryan Chapell (speech, Berean Baptist Church, Livonia, Michigan, May 3–4, 2013).

6. C. S. Lewis, *Mere Christianity*, The Complete C. S. Lewis Signature Classics (New York: HarperCollins, 2012), 192.

CHAPTER 6: SET FREE *FOR FREEDOM FROM GUILT*

1. Francis Thompson, *The Hound of Heaven* (Portland, ME: Thomas Bird Mosher, 1917), 3.

2. John F. MacArthur, *New Testament Commentary: First Corinthians* (Chicago: Moody Bible Institute, 1984), 192.

3. Elyse Fitzpatrick (speech, Liberate Conference, Coral Ridge Presbyterian Church, Fort Lauderdale, FL, February 19–21, 2015).

4. Preserved Smith, *The Life and Letters of Martin Luther* (Boston: Houghton Mifflin, 1914), 324–25.

CHAPTER 7: SET FREE *FOR FREEDOM FROM SHAME*

1. David Powlison and Julie Lowe, interviewed by Andrew Ray, "What Is the Difference between Guilt and Shame?," CCEF, podcast audio, January 18, 2012, www.ccef.org/resources/podcast/what-difference-between-guilt -and-shame.

2. Walter A. Elwell and Barry J. Beitzel, *Baker Encyclopedia of the Bible* (Grand Rapids, MI: Baker, 1988), 1087.

3. According to Borchert, "The patriarch Jacob was not only an ancestor revered by the Jews but also by the Samaritans. Although there is no Old Testament text that relates Jacob to this well, it was part of the region's tradition. The woman's question, therefore, of whether Jesus was greater than their ancestor Jacob, who provided the historic well, raised the issue of the common ancestry of Jew and Samaritan." Gerald L. Borchert, *The New American Commentary: John 1–11*, vol. 25 (Nashville: B&H, 1996), 204–5.

4. Stephen Um, "The Secure Leader" (speech, Healthy Leaders Conference, Dallas, November 12–14, 2015), Acts29.com, accessed July 27, 2016, www.acts29.com/session-3-the-secure-leader/.

CHAPTER 8: SET FREE *FOR FREEDOM TO SAY YES*

1. Sarah McLachlan, "Adia," *Surfacing* © 1997 Arista Records.

2. Ray C. Stedman, "When the Spirit Says No," RayStedman.org, accessed July 27, 2016, www.raystedman.org/new-testament/1-john/when-the-spirit -says-no.

3. I'm pretty sure I heard Matt Chandler say this once, but I am getting old, so maybe I just thought he did. Sure sounds like him.

CHAPTER 9: SET FREE *TO LOVE*

1. John Piper, as quoted in "Tozer's Contradiction and His Approach to Piety," Gospel Coalition, June 8, 2008, http://blogs.thegospelcoalition.org /justintaylor/2008/06/08/tozers-contradiction-and-his-approach_08/.

2. Justin Holcomb, "How 'Love God and Others' Is a Backward Gospel," JustinHolcomb.com, June 11, 2012, http://justinholcomb.com/2012/ 06/11/how-love-god-and-others-is-a-backward-gospel/.

CHAPTER 10: SET FREE *TO LIVE FREE*

1. The original article I read was from *60 Minutes*: Anderson Cooper, "North Korean Prisoner Escaped after Twenty-Three Brutal Years," December 2, 2012, www.cbsnews.com/news/north-korean-prisoner-escaped-after-23 -brutal-years-15-05-2013/. Since the release of the article, Shin has admitted some of the details were inaccurate (Anna Fifield, "Prominent North Korean Defector Shin Dong-hyuk Admits Parts of Story Are Inaccurate," *Washington Post*, January 17, 2015, www.washingtonpost.com/world/prominent -n-korean-defector-shin-dong-hyuk-admits-parts-of-story-are-inaccurate /2015/01/17/fc69278c-9dd5-11e4-bcfb-059ec7a93ddc_story.html), but none of the portions of the story I refer to were fabricated or altered. You can read about his entire ordeal in the book *Escape from Camp 14: One Man's Remarkable Odyssey from North Korea to Freedom in the West* by Blaine Harden (New York: Penguin, 2013).

2. Steve Brown, "Mirror and Picture," *You Think about That*, May 2, 2016, www.keylife.org/shows/mirror-picture.